1 0 0

Favorite

Perennials

100
FAVORITE
PERENNIALS

TERI DUNN

MetroBooks

DEDICATION

For my nephew Josh, a true hardy perennial

MetroBooks

An Imprint of Friedman/Fairfax Publishers

© 1998 by Michael Friedman Publishing Group, Inc.

Library of Congress Cataloging-in-Publication Data

Dunn, Teri.
    100 favorite perennials / Teri Dunn.
        p.   cm.
    ISBN 1-56799-527-6
    1. Perennials.   I. Title. II. Title: One hundred favorite perennials.
    SB434.D86   1997
    635.9'32- - DC20   96-34520

Editor: Susan Lauzau
Art Director: Lynne Yeamans
Designer: Milagros Sensat
Photography Editor: Wendy Missan
Production Manager: Karen Greenberg

Color separations by Ocean Graphic Co. Ltd.
Printed in Singapore by KHL Pte Co. Ltd.

For bulk purchases and special sales, please contact:
Friedman/Fairfax Publishers
Attention: Sales Department
15 West 26th Street
New York, NY 10010
212/685-6610 FAX 212/685-1307

Visit our website:
http://www.metrobooks.com

Photography credits:

©R. Todd Davis: 16, 18, 20, 22, 23, 24, 27, 28, 29, 34, 42, 65, 74, 76, 78, 81, 85, 91, 95, 103

©Alan & Linda Detrick: 66, 102

©Derek Fell: 13, 57, 94, 104, 111, 113, 115, 117

©Pamela Harper: 44, 53

©Dency Kane: 2, 8, 17, 19, 21, 25, 26, 31, 32, 33, 39, 40, 41, 45, 47, 50, 56, 67, 69, 70, 72, 80, 82, 87, 88, 89, 92, 93, 97, 101

©Charles Mann: 12, 15, 30, 35, 37, 38, 48, 49, 51, 52, 54, 60, 61, 62, 63, 64, 68, 71, 73, 77, 79, 83, 84, 90, 98, 105, 107, 109, 110, 112, 114

©Jerry Pavia: 10, 14, 36, 46, 59, 86, 96, 100, 106, 116

Photo/Nats, Inc.: ©Kim Blaxland: 75; ©Syaney Karp: 43; ©John A. Lynch: 99; ©Robert E. Lyons: 11, 55; ©Cann Reilly: 58

©Nancy Truworthy: 7

CONTENTS

Introduction

Gardening with perennials can be a great joy. Once planted, they bring wonderful color, texture, and form to your garden for years to come. In the end, they're more gratifying to grow than "flash in the pan" annuals that need to be repurchased and replanted every year. With perennials, you have a lot to look forward to as they mature, spread or billow out, and reach their full character. Perennials are an investment, and when well chosen and well nurtured, they'll repay you handsomely, transforming your garden into a showpiece.

There are many, many perennials in the world. This book highlights one hundred of the easiest and most dependable, taking the uncertainty out of your first purchases. None is rare or hard to find. Study the descriptions as well as the photographs, decide which ones are right for you, and rest easy. You're off to a good start.

SHOPPING FOR PERENNIALS

When you buy your perennials locally, you can take them right home and plant them the same day. If you join the mobs down at the local garden center the first warm Saturday in spring, however, be prepared to accept substitutes for the exact perennials you had in mind. You should

return in the less-hectic autumn, which, unknown to some gardeners, is also a great time to plant. The soil is still warm and, when the rains come, the roots will grow quickly and give the plants a head start over their spring-planted counterparts. Another advantage to a follow-up autumn shopping trip is that you'll be armed with a summertime of experience and may shop more wisely.

In any case, the secret to being a savvy garden center shopper is taking your time. Draw up a shopping list beforehand so you don't get overwhelmed by all the choices (though you may still end up making an impulse purchase or two) or the jostling crowds. Examine each plant carefully. Check to see that it's well rooted by turning it over or sideways and thumping the pot lightly. Neither the plant nor the soil mix should fall out, and you may see a few roots peeking out of the drainage holes. Make sure that it's pest-free— look on leaf undersides and in the nodes (where stalks meet stem) for small bugs, sticky residue, or webs. And check that it's disease-free—no spotted, curled, or yellowed leaves, or deformed buds. Don't be seduced by a blooming plant, as the petals may drop on the car ride home or after a few days in your garden. Better to buy a plant that's full of unopened buds, or at least showing signs of fresh, new green growth.

Another option is to buy your perennials from a reputable mail-order catalog; see the list of sources on page 119. You'll find a far wider range of plants and individual cultivars, plus information and inspiring landscaping ideas—more than you can hope to find at a busy garden center. Mail-order perennials tend to come in two forms:

potted and bareroot. Potted ones are generally small (to keep shipping costs down), but don't let size deceive you. They may be one- to two-year-old, well-rooted plants whose foliage has just been chopped back. Once in the ground, they often take off like gangbusters. Bareroot selections offer the further advantage of arriving dormant, so you can plant them a little earlier and let them ease into life in your garden gradually. One last note: always read catalog fine print carefully so you are aware not only of what you are getting but also of substitution and guarantee policies.

As you get more involved in raising perennials, you may wish to save money—or try some rare plants—by growing from seed. There are good books available on seed-starting techniques, but be aware that it can sometimes be an elaborate process. Special harvesting methods, soil mixes, and chilling and warming cycles may be necessary, depending on the plant. It can also be a slow process, taking months or even years. And finally, not all perennials "come true" from seed. An easy, quick way to get carbon copies of perennials you enjoy is by division (see page 9).

PLANTING PERENNIALS

The best thing you can do for your new perennials is prepare the soil ahead of time. Assuming you've picked an appropriate spot in sun or shade, the next step is to improve the bed's quality and texture. Most perennials want a well-drained soil, which means a soil that is neither boggy nor too sandy. To get well-drained soil, dig in some organic matter (compost or rotted cow manure is always a good choice) to a depth of 6 to 12 inches (15 to 30cm). Keep stress to a minimum by planting in the late afternoon, on a gray or rainy day, if possible. And be prepared to protect the young plant from wind, hot sun, and pests like hungry slugs or birds until it gets established. Anything from chicken-wire cylinders to a "fortress" of plywood scraps may be used.

If your plant is a bareroot, soak it for an hour or two in a bucket of water to rehydrate it. If you're planting a potted perennial, gently pop it out of its container just before planting time. In either case, take a few moments to groom the plant first, snipping off dead or damaged roots or stems. Then place it in an ample hole, firm soil around it, and water it in well.

CARING FOR PERENNIALS

While every plant has its own specific needs, there are general guidelines you can follow for the care and feeding of most perennials. Be sure to water, especially during the first season while the roots are getting established. Don't count on rain and don't wait until you see alarming wilting; water often and generously. Water at the plant's base (this gets to the roots quickly and keeps the foliage dry, which prevents disease). Also, feed your new plants! Mix a standard soluble fertilizer like 5-10-5 in with their water once or twice a month during the growing season. Or sprinkle granular food at their bases and water in well, again once or twice a month. Always follow the label directions so you don't overfeed or undernourish. Your perennials will reward you with lusty new growth and lush blooms—and you will build a foundation for a healthy, solid, and gorgeous performance in years to come.

If you keep up with routine chores in your flower garden, you'll help your perennials prosper and save yourself extra work down the line. Always remove weeds, particularly in the vulnerable first year. Not only are they unsightly, they sap the precious food and water that your plants need to thrive.

Every few days nip out blooms that have passed. This keeps your perennials looking attractive, and it gives them extra energy for more blooming (rather than spending their efforts on going to seed). Harvesting an occasional bouquet can also inspire a plant to bloom some more!

After a few years in the garden, your perennials may become crowded and cease to bloom or grow as well. This is a sure sign that it's time to divide. Most perennials should be divided in the spring or autumn—summer is just too stressful. Simply dig up a plant, taking care to get as much of the root system as possible. Split it into sections, making sure that each section has "growing points" (eyes visible on the rootstock or viable roots with some healthy growth attached). Bare hands alone may not do the trick; you may have to resort to slicing or chopping with a sharp knife, trowel, or shovel. Then, replant the pieces in the same spot or elsewhere in your garden, allowing each one plenty of elbow room. If you have too many, give some away to your neighbors.

If, despite all your kind treatment, your perennials begin to suffer from what appears to be a disease or pest infestation, act quickly. Remove affected foliage and flowers from the plant and from the ground at its feet, and destroy them. Pick off larger bugs and drown them in soapy water, and knock off little ones with a spray of the hose. If the problem remains, you need to move on to diagnosis and treatment. Look up the symptoms in a book, or take a bug or afflicted sample to a more experienced gardener or a good garden center. If you find you must spray your perennials, always use a product that is labeled specifically for the problem, and always follow the directions on the label to the letter.

UNDERSTANDING HARDINESS

First-time perennial gardeners are often bewildered by plant hardiness zones. Don't worry: it's really a simple system, based on the lowest average winter temperatures in different areas. Some perennials are better than others at surviving cold and freezing weather.

First you need to determine which zone you are in (see map on page 118). Then select perennials that are described as hardy in your zone. You can feel confident that these perennials will make it through the winter and live to bloom again next year. Some gardeners take chances; for example, they'll grow a Zone 5 plant in the more northerly Zone 4. If you have a protected warm pocket or spot on your property, and you mulch the plant well in autumn, it may just make it through. Conversely, a Zone 7 plant may survive a steamy Zone 9 or 10 summer if it gets some extra shade and water during the heat of the day.

A little trial and error will teach you about getting your perennials through the winter. Depending on the plants and where you live, some can be chopped back each autumn and left alone until they revive at the return of spring. Others need protection; if an insulating blanket of snow cannot be counted on, and even if it can, mulching is often wise. Wait until late autumn, then lay down several inches of bark mulch, straw, chopped leaves, or evergreen boughs. Don't forget to remove the covering in spring when the soil begins to warm up again and you spot new growth emerging.

Acanthus mollis

Bear's-breeches, acanthus

BLOOM TIME: late spring–summer

HEIGHT/WIDTH: 3'–4' × 2' (90–120cm × 60cm)

LIGHT: full sun–partial shade

ZONES: 7–10

Bear's-breeches

This splendid, clump-forming plant has long been treasured for its big, handsome leaves, which can reach up to 2 feet (60cm) long and half as wide. They're dark green, lustrous, and tough, with deep lobes. You may recognize their bold and elegant form from renderings in art, fabrics, and decorations, and from patterned Corinthian columns.

In fact, acanthus is native to the Mediterranean and grows wild in Greece. It thrives and is more likely to flower in warmer zones in North America. But it may need a little shade in the heat of the day. The bicolor flowers—creamy white with mauve bracts—appear along stiff stalks that rise to about 4 or 5 feet (1.2 or 1.5m) above the foliage.

A plant this imposing needs plenty of elbow room. It makes a great focal point in a flower border, in a tub on a deck, or lining a path or steps. Just be sure to plant it where you want it to stay, because its root system is robust, and you'll never completely remove it if you try to transplant it. Its only enemies are slugs and snails, which can disfigure the gorgeous leaves and spoil their majestic appearance. Make sure it has well-drained soil.

Achillea filipendulina

Yarrow

BLOOM TIME: summer

HEIGHT/WIDTH: 3½'–4' × 1½'–2' (105–120cm × 45–60cm)

LIGHT: full sun

ZONES: 3–8

Yarrow

Achillea has everything going for it: attractive, ferny, olive green foliage, loads of pretty flowers that stay in bloom for weeks, and an agreeable disposition. It adores full sun, and, once established, is drought-tolerant. It is not fussy about soil, growing quickly and lustily in any well-drained spot. (Note that rich or damp soil leads to spindly growth and small flowers.)

The flat-topped blooms, generally 5 inches (13cm) across, are actually tight clusters of tiny flowers. 'Gold Plate' is well named, with slightly larger bright yellow flower heads on a taller plant (to 5 feet [1.5m]) that may need staking. The softer-hued 'Coronation Gold' is smaller (to 3 feet [90cm]) because it's a hybrid between *Achillea filipendulina* and a shorter relative. You'll also find individuals and mixes in pretty shades of white, pink, and salmon-orange; these are also hybrids.

All achilleas are great in sweeps, clumps, or interspersed throughout a flower border where you want dependable color. You'll have plenty for cutting; they're also wonderful for dried flower arrangements.

Aconitum napellus

Common monkshood

BLOOM TIME: summer–late summer

HEIGHT/WIDTH: 3' × 2' (90 × 60cm)

LIGHT: full sun–partial shade

ZONES: 4–8

Common monkshood

Gorgeous spikes of these blue-violet, helmet-shaped flowers appear in late summer, when they are a welcome sight. The divided leaves are attractive, remaining dark green all season and alternating up the stem to just short of the flowers. The plants have an airy, graceful quality. They blend well with other perennials of medium height and will give your yard a nice, cottage garden feel. Their most important requirement is rich, moist (but not soggy) soil.

There are many cultivars and closely related species. In particular, look for the hybrids, including the dense, long-blooming 'Bressingham Spire' and the tall, vivid blue 'Spark's Variety'.

Much has been made of the fact that all the plant parts, especially the roots, are deadly poisonous. The only death-by-aconitum story that comes readily to mind, however, is Romeo in Shakespeare's play. Still, it would be wise to grow this plant out of the reach of curious children.

Agapanthus

Agapanthus

BLOOM TIME: summer–early autumn

HEIGHT/WIDTH: 2½'–4' × 2' (75–120cm × 60cm)

LIGHT: full sun

ZONES: 8–10

'Headbourne' agapanthus

Long a favorite in California gardens, where it grows so well, this terrific "tender perennial" really deserves a chance in other regions. It will grow well in soil of poor-to-average fertility, is drought-tolerant, and blooms for weeks during the first half of the summer. If you have doubts about its ability to survive your winters, grow some in pots and move the plants indoors for the cold months.

The straplike leaves appear first, from the base of the plant. They are later joined by bare stalks bearing show-off flower heads that are between 5 and 8 inches (13 and 20.5cm) across. Composed of small, tubular flowers, these may be loose and carefree, or dense and spherical enough to invite comparison to a flowering allium.

You'll find these plants in a variety of shades of blue and purple, as well as white. The hardiest ones may be the English Headbourne Hybrids, which grow a little shorter and stouter. Newer varieties have been bred to produce loads of flowering stalks—look for the aptly named 'Prolific Blue' and 'Prolific White'.

Ajuga reptans

Bugleweed

BLOOM TIME: late spring–early summer

HEIGHT/WIDTH: 4"–8" × 8" (10–20cm × 20cm)

LIGHT: full sun–full shade

ZONES: 4–8

'Catlin's Giant' bugleweed

An adaptable, fast-spreading (some say invasive) choice for shade, this mat-former will fill in where grass languishes—but will also do perfectly well in sun. It comes in a variety of intriguing forms; if you search the nurseries or catalogs diligently, you can find a handsome, unusual, low-maintenance planting.

The small spike flowers, which appear in profusion in late spring, are usually purple. They look very much like those of mint, which is no surprise, as this plant is a relative. The flowers tend to dry to a dull brown, so keep the display attractive by clipping them off when their looks start to fade.

Among the many choices are 'Burgundy Glow', whose leaves are splashed with pink and cream; 'Pink Surprise', with lance-shaped, bronze-green leaves (and pinkish flowers); and 'Purple Brocade', which sports especially ruffled, duo-tone leaves of purple-bronze and forest green. The most intriguing cultivar is bronze-foliaged 'Catlin's Giant', which has extra-large leaves and taller flowers. (It originated in the garden of a fellow who accidentally sprayed weed-killer on his ajuga patch. Most of the plants died, but one clump survived and came back in this jumbo size.)

Alcea rosea

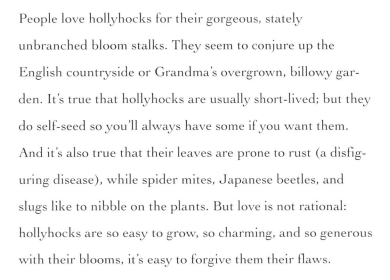

Hollyhock

BLOOM TIME: summer–autumn

HEIGHT/WIDTH: 5'–10' × 3' (1.5–3m × 90cm)

LIGHT: full sun

ZONES: 5–9

Hollyhock

People love hollyhocks for their gorgeous, stately unbranched bloom stalks. They seem to conjure up the English countryside or Grandma's overgrown, billowy garden. It's true that hollyhocks are usually short-lived; but they do self-seed so you'll always have some if you want them. And it's also true that their leaves are prone to rust (a disfiguring disease), while spider mites, Japanese beetles, and slugs like to nibble on the plants. But love is not rational: hollyhocks are so easy to grow, so charming, and so generous with their blooms, it's easy to forgive them their flaws.

Classic hollyhock clumps can grow quite tall, up to 8 feet (2.4m) or more. Their impressive height makes them perfect for planting at the back of a border or along a fence or wall, where you can admire them swaying in a soft summer breeze. A wide range of colors is available, from white to yellow to pink to lavender. There's even a deep maroon cultivar ('Nigra' or 'The Watchman') that's nearly black. Old-fashioned favorites have single blooms, and more recent "double" cultivars are so fluffy with petals that they look almost like peony blossoms.

Alchemilla mollis

Lady's-mantle

BLOOM TIME: late spring–early summer

HEIGHT/WIDTH: 1'–2' × 1½' (30–60cm × 45cm)

LIGHT: full sun–partial shade

ZONES: 4–7

Lady's-mantle

Every garden should have a spot for this lovely, lush plant, whether it's used as a groundcover, part of the perennial border, or featured in a handsome urn or terra-cotta pot. The scalloped leaves (up to 4 inches [10cm] wide) are lime green and soft to the touch. When it rains or when early morning dew gathers on the leaves, the water beads up like quicksilver and sparkles—a truly enchanting sight.

Unlike some other foliage plants, lady's-mantle has attractive flowers. The frothy flowers are a sharp, clear shade of yellow-green (often described as chartreuse), and appear in profusion each spring. They grow on short stalks that hold them slightly away from the leaves.

Lady's-mantle is easy to grow and adapts well to both sun and partial shade. Just be sure that it gets well-drained but moist soil. If your summers are hot and dry, coddle the plants with fertile soil, some shade, and extra water.

Amsonia tabernaemontana

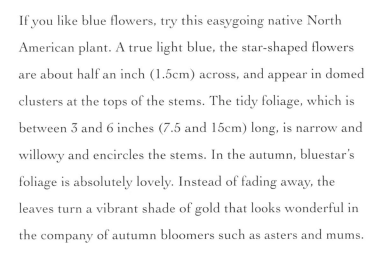

Bluestar

BLOOM TIME: early summer

HEIGHT/WIDTH: 2'–3' × 2' 3' (60–90cm × 60–90cm)

LIGHT: full sun–partial shade

ZONES: 3–9

Bluestar

If you like blue flowers, try this easygoing native North American plant. A true light blue, the star-shaped flowers are about half an inch (1.5cm) across, and appear in domed clusters at the tops of the stems. The tidy foliage, which is between 3 and 6 inches (7.5 and 15cm) long, is narrow and willowy and encircles the stems. In the autumn, bluestar's foliage is absolutely lovely. Instead of fading away, the leaves turn a vibrant shade of gold that looks wonderful in the company of autumn bloomers such as asters and mums.

Surprisingly strong and tough, these plants stand erect and thrive in moderately fertile soil. (They can be grown in some shade and in richer soil, but will become leggy and need to be trimmed back occasionally to keep their growth dense.) They're also free of disease and pest problems. Bluestar is probably best grown in groups or sweeps, where its fine texture won't be lost and the wonderful shade of blue really stands out. It's also a striking companion for orange- or red-flowered azaleas, which bloom at the same time.

Anemone × hybrida

Japanese anemone

BLOOM TIME: late summer–autumn

HEIGHT/WIDTH: 3'–5' × 2' (90–150cm × 60cm)

LIGHT: full sun–partial shade

ZONES: 5–8

'Queen Charlotte' Japanese anemone

When your autumn garden needs some pizzazz, consider late-blooming, low-maintenance Japanese anemones. They're as fresh as daisies, which they resemble from a distance, and as graceful as old-fashioned single-form roses, which they resemble up close. The plants grow into substantial mounds laden with attractive compound foliage. The 2- to 4-inch (5 to 10 cm) flowers surge above, held high on arching stalks. Occasionally this plant is called windflower: the clouds of flower stalks being tossed gently in an autumn breeze is an irresistible sight. Tuck some into your flower borders, among ornamental grasses, or in a bed with other autumn bloomers. There are several good cultivars available. The white ones are old favorites: 'Honorine Jobert', first introduced in 1858, stands 3 to 4 feet (90 to 120cm) tall; 'Alba' is about a foot shorter, and just as breathtaking. Another short one to look for is 'September Charm', which tops out at between 2 and 3 feet (60 and 90cm), and has unusual rose-pink flowers with a silvery sheen. For best results, Japanese anemones require soil that is moist and rich in organic matter.

Anthemis tinctoria

Golden marguerite

BLOOM TIME: late spring–early autumn

HEIGHT/WIDTH: 1½'–3' × 2½' (45–90cm × 75cm)

LIGHT: full sun

ZONES: 3–7

'E.C. Buxton' golden marguerite

A true yellow-flowered daisy, golden marguerite is an enthusiastic, low-maintenance plant. It produces loads of small flowers—no more than 2 inches (5cm) across—for up to two months running. Give it a spot in full sun and lean soil. And be sure to trim off spent flowers occasionally to encourage continued blooming. Or, better yet, cut bouquets for yourself fairly often. The plant is rather bushy and sprawling, and clothed in ferny, divided daisy foliage. Once established, it will be quite drought-resistant.

Because of its casual appearance, this easygoing plant is a good companion for herbs. But it really looks terrific in the company of blue or red flowers, like 'Johnson's Blue' geranium or any of the red-hued bee balms. No pests ever bother it, and mildew only appears when air circulation is poor, a problem easily remedied by giving it plenty of elbow room.

Aquilegia × hybrida

Columbine

BLOOM TIME: spring–early summer

HEIGHT/WIDTH: 2'–3' × 1½' (60–90cm × 45cm)

LIGHT: full sun–partial shade

ZONES: 3–9

Columbine

The original red-and-yellow wild columbine (*A. canadensis*), simple to grow and long popular with gardeners, has now been joined by a host of fabulous, tall, multicolored hybrids. Their charm is owed to their intriguing flower form—five sepals centered by a boss of perky yellow stamens and backed by five true petals that are usually spurred. Some of the varieties have flowers that nod, and most columbines have sepals and spurs of contrasting colors, which make for a lively display.

Perhaps the best of the lot are the McKana Giants, which grow between 2 and 3 feet (60 and 90cm) tall. They carry lots of extra-large flowers in cream-and-yellow, pink-and-white,

lilac-and-yellow, and other combinations. The durable 'Biedermeier' strain is about half as tall, and has shorter spurs, but comes in an equally diverse color range. If you prefer solid-color columbines, there are plenty of choices, from sherbet yellow 'Maxistar' to pristine white 'Snow Queen'. All are splendid performers in perennial borders.

Columbine's only flaw is that its lacy foliage is prone to leaf miners, which weave their trails inside the leaves until little green is left. The flowers keep on blooming though, seemingly unaffected. Remove all damaged foliage, or wait until flowering is over and cut the entire plant down. A fresh flush of new foliage will appear shortly after.

Arabis caucasica

Rock cress

BLOOM TIME: spring

HEIGHT/WIDTH: 6"–9" × 1' (15–23cm × 30cm)

LIGHT: full sun

ZONES: 4–7

'Spring Charm' rock cress

Some rock garden plants are too fussy for beginning gardeners to bother with, but rock cress will give your garden that elfin look with little trouble. It's an obliging plant, forming a neat, low-growing mat of gray-green 1-inch (2.5cm) leaves that are woolly to the touch. Spring brings stalks (up to 1 foot [30cm] high) of small flowers. The species is a crisp white; the cultivar 'Flore Pleno' has dense, double, longer-lasting white flowers. There is also a pink single-flowered version, named 'Spring Charm'.

Rock cress is happiest in full sun and well-drained soil. It sulks in humid summers. To encourage denser growth, trim back the entire plant after flowering.

Try this plant along a walkway or rock wall. Or you may wish to include it in your bed of spring-flowering bulbs; its delicate flowers will be good company, and the foliage will remain to help distract from the dying-back bulb leaves as summer approaches.

Armeria maritima

Thrift, sea pink

BLOOM TIME: late spring–early summer

HEIGHT/WIDTH: 6"–1' × 1½' (15–30cm × 45cm)

LIGHT: full sun

ZONES: 4–8

'Dusseldorf Pride' thrift

As the name *maritima* suggests, this is a good plant for a seaside garden or, indeed, for any garden with sandy soil. The foliage is fine and dense, almost like grass. It forms little tufted mounds that don't sprawl out much, so it looks good in rock garden settings or in front of other plants as an edging.

The gorgeous flowers appear in profusion just above the foliage in spring, with occasional repeats throughout the summer. These perky 1-inch (2.5cm) balls, borne on bare stalks, look like little flowering alliums. The most popular form is white 'Alba', which mixes well with spring bulbs and other early-flowering perennials. There are also pink cultivars, including the vibrant (and dauntingly named) 'Vindictive' and a stunning new red cultivar called 'Dusseldorf Pride'.

Artemisia

Wormwood, mugwort

BLOOM TIME: spring–summer
(not grown for its flowers)

HEIGHT/WIDTH: varies

LIGHT: full sun

ZONES: 4–8

'Silver King' wormwood

There are more than two hundred species of artemisia, but many are too rangy for use in gardens. Luckily, horticulturists have recognized the value of the silvery foliage, the ease of culture and dependability, and, in many cases, the wonderful, sagelike scent. Today, we can choose from a number of improved selections. The most widely grown is probably *A. schmidtiana* 'Silver Mound', whose thin, silky leaves grow closely to form a compact clump up to 1 foot (30cm) high and at least that wide. Ideal for edging, it also mixes well in the flower border. It looks especially good in the company of purple, blue, and lavender blooms. For taller, lacy plants that blend in beautifully with perennials of similar height, try the

A. ludoviciana cultivars: 'Silver King' is 3 feet (90cm) tall; 'Silver Queen' is 2 feet (60cm) tall; and 'Valerie Finnis', between 2 and 3 feet (60 and 90cm) tall with broader leaves. *A. stellerana* 'Silver Brocade' looks a lot like dusty miller, but is perennial. Note that artemisia is grown for its foliage; the small white or yellowish flowers are nothing to write home about, and are best clipped off.

All of these artemisias do well in poor-to-medium soil, and can spread if you don't keep after them. They keep their cool in the heat of summer, look lovely among pastel flowers, make bright flowers seem more vibrant, and flatter dark green foliage. No garden should be without them.

Aruncus
dioicus

Goatsbeard

BLOOM TIME: early summer

HEIGHT/WIDTH: 4'–7' × 3'–4' (1.2–2.1m × 90–120cm)

LIGHT: full sun–partial shade

ZONES: 2–6

Goatsbeard

This shrublike plant has a short moment of glory, but what a show! Great, stately, feathery wands of creamy white flowers bloom for a week or two in early summer. Rising above the light green foliage, they look for all the world like big astilbe blossoms. The male and female flowers are borne on separate plants and the male flowers are fuller. Unfortunately, nurseries don't differentiate and you won't know what you have until it blooms. Staking isn't necessary.

When grown in the partial shade it prefers, goatsbeard lights up the scene like few other shade bloomers can,

thanks to its size. It's dazzling in a woodland garden, and can also be grown out in the open, provided the soil is constantly moist.

After the flowers pass, you'll still appreciate the plant for its foliage. The delicate, textured leaves are compound, dissected, toothed, and clothe the plant from head to toe. They are untroubled by pests and look fresh all season. If the species is too big for your purposes, seek out the shorter cultivars 'Child of Two Worlds' (3 to 4 feet [90 to 120cm]) or 'Kneiffii' (3 feet [90cm]).

Asarum europaeum

European wild ginger

BLOOM TIME: spring (not grown for its flowers)

HEIGHT/WIDTH: 5"–6" × 8"–1' (13–15cm × 20.5–30cm)

LIGHT: partial–full shade

ZONES: 4–7

European wild ginger

If your yard has a shady spot with moist soil, you already know that not much will grow there. Time to turn it over to this fast-growing, glossy-leaved, tidy groundcover—you'll be delighted with the transformation. There are other wild gingers, but European wild ginger is the choicest and easiest to grow. The kidney-shaped leaves are uniform, about 2 to 3 inches (5 to 7.5cm) across, and evergreen in most parts of North America. Carried on short stems, they're thick, leathery, and shiny, retaining their crisp look even in the heat of summer. Tiny brownish or purplish flowers appear in the spring, but they get lost under the foliage and aren't especially noteworthy anyway.

European wild ginger forms a full carpet. You may wish to inject a few shade-loving companions in its midst, such as a groundcovering phlox or some dwarf hostas. Or try pairing it with smaller spring-flowering bulbs, such as scilla or crocus. The ginger leaves will cover over the fading foliage after the bulbs have bloomed.

Aster novae-angliae

Michaelmas daisy, New England aster

BLOOM TIME: late summer–autumn

HEIGHT/WIDTH: 3'–6½' × 2'–3' (90cm–1.9m × 60–90cm)

LIGHT: full sun

ZONES: 4–8

'Purple Dome' Michaelmas daisy

Late summer and early autumn wouldn't be complete without exuberant blooming asters. There are plenty to choose from, but the very best are the Michaelmas daisies, selections of *Aster novae-angliae*. Ironically, a number of these were bred in Europe from native North American species—a case of European gardeners spotting potential where we only saw weeds. 'Alma Potschke' is a splendid plant, sporting gorgeous 2- to 3-inch (5 to 7.5cm) rosy pink blooms with bright yellow centers. Growing up to 4 feet (1.2m) tall, it may need staking. At 20 inches (51cm) tall, 'Purple Dome' is a more compact prize. As its name suggests, this cultivar becomes covered with flowers, to the point of nearly obscuring the foliage. The flowers are approximately 2 inches (5cm) across, and a rich dark purple with a contrasting yellow center. And there are many others, all of which stay in bloom for several weeks running.

Michaelmas daisy selections are robust plants, forming clumps and developing woody stems. The leaves are lance-shaped, and the lower ones tend to drop, leaving the plant bare-kneed. If this bothers you, plant something shorter in front of them.

Astilbe × arendsii

Astilbe

BLOOM TIME: varies; early–late summer

HEIGHT/WIDTH: 1½'–4' × 1½'–2½' (45–120cm × 45–75cm)

LIGHT: partial shade–full sun

ZONES: 4–9

'Deutchland' astilbe

Astilbes are among the finest of the shade-loving perennials. But they require rich, moist, well-drained soil, and must be grown in areas not given to extremes of heat or humidity. Many of the best varieties were bred in Germany at the turn of the century by accomplished plantsman George Arends. The magnificent feathery plumes, actually a mass of tiny flowers, come in a range of colors, from white to lavender to pink to red.

Planted in a sweep in a woodland setting or even as a formal circle around the base of a tree, astilbes are delightful. You can try them in full sun, too, so long as they still get plenty of moisture. They're a popular choice for along the banks of a pond, stream, or pool.

After the flowers go by, the plant remains attractive. A clump-former, it is clothed in toothed leaflets that look somewhat ferny. Problems with diseases and pests are rare.

Aurinia saxatilis

Basket-of-gold

BLOOM TIME: spring

HEIGHT/WIDTH: 1'–2' × 1' (30–60cm × 30cm)

LIGHT: full sun

ZONES: 3–7

Basket-of-gold

Basket-of-gold looks like it should be easy to grow, and it is. It loves to spill over walls, to froth over the edge of containers, window boxes, or raised beds, and to weave its cheerful color into the early-season garden. A trailing, sprawling plant, it bears cluster after cluster of densely packed, tiny yellow flowers. (They may remind you of their relatives—the mustard flowers that coat hillsides in California in the spring and summer.) For variation, you could grow 'Citrinum', which has lemon yellow flowers, or the more recent introduction, 'Sunny Border Apricot', whose blooms have a peachy hue.

The profuse flowers nearly blanket the fuzzy, gray-green leaves. After blooming is over, the hummock form can get a bit rangy and ratty looking, especially if your summers are humid. Step in with your clippers and chop the plants back by about a third, and they'll return in full glory next spring.

Baptisia australis

False indigo, false blue indigo

BLOOM TIME: early summer

HEIGHT/WIDTH: 3'–6' × 3' (90cm–1.8m × 90cm)

LIGHT: full sun–partial shade

ZONES: 3–9

False indigo

This shrubby perennial has blue-green foliage and 10-inch (25.5cm) spikes of lavender-blue flowers that stay in bloom for up to a month. A member of the pea family, there is a resemblance both in the leaflets and in the classic flower form to other members of this family — including sweet peas and lupines.

Super-easy to grow, false indigo requires only well-drained soil; it does well in poor-to-average soil. Just be sure to place it where you want it to stay, because it forms a deep taproot that makes later transplanting an ordeal. False indigo holds its own in a formal flower border, but is equally at home in a more casual, cottage garden setting. It is disease- and pest-free.

When the flowers fade, they are replaced by brown, pendulous pods. Some people harvest the pods for dried flower arrangements or as rattling toys for a cat. But you can also coax the plant into blooming longer if you cut off the blooms before they go to seed.

Bergenia cordifolia

Heart-leaved bergenia

BLOOM TIME: spring

HEIGHT/WIDTH: 1'–1½' × 1' (30–45cm × 30cm)

LIGHT: partial shade

ZONES: 3–8

Heart-leaved bergenia

Bergenia forms big, bold cabbagelike clumps with sturdy, glossy leaves. The oval or heart-shaped leaves can be up to 1 foot (30cm) across; while they look almost tropical, the plants are very hardy. Leathery and shiny, the leaves can develop brown edges if you expose them to too much sun in the summer or if you neglect to mulch for a harsh winter. Otherwise, the plant is handsome in all seasons, remaining evergreen in most areas. The onset of cool autumn weather inspires the leaves to turn an attractive shade of bronze, russet, or purple. Heart-leaved bergenia is a dramatic choice for mass plantings; try it under a tree or at the base of a shrub border.

In the spring, lush trusses of pink blossoms appear on strong stalks just above the leaves. There are a number of worthy hybrids. 'Abendglut' ('Evening Glow') has nearly crimson flowers and foliage that turns maroon in winter. 'Perfecta' has rosy red flowers and purplish leaves. And 'Silberlicht' ('Silver Light') has pink-blushed white flowers with red centers.

Boltonia asteroides

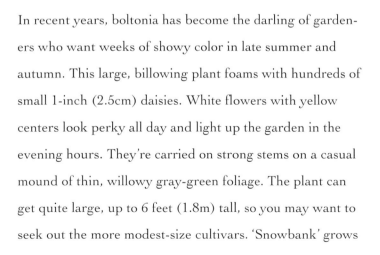

Boltonia

BLOOM TIME: late summer–autumn

HEIGHT/WIDTH: 4'–6' × 2'–4' (1.2–1.8m × 60–120cm)

LIGHT: full sun

ZONES: 4–9

'Snowbank' boltonia

In recent years, boltonia has become the darling of gardeners who want weeks of showy color in late summer and autumn. This large, billowing plant foams with hundreds of small 1-inch (2.5cm) daisies. White flowers with yellow centers look perky all day and light up the garden in the evening hours. They're carried on strong stems on a casual mound of thin, willowy gray-green foliage. The plant can get quite large, up to 6 feet (1.8m) tall, so you may want to seek out the more modest-size cultivars. 'Snowbank' grows to between 3 and 4 feet (90 and 120cm). 'Pink Beauty' has pink flowers and grows to about the same size.

An easy plant to grow, boltonia requires only plenty of sun. If the soil is naturally moist and fertile, the plant will prosper for years with little attention. It does well even in drier soils, though it may not grow as tall or lush. Only the species will need staking. Grow it with yellow flowers for a pretty picture: try garden-variety goldenrods, sneezeweed, or one of the smaller-flowered sunflowers.

Brunnera macrophylla

Siberian bugloss, perennial forget-me-not

BLOOM TIME: late spring–early summer

HEIGHT/WIDTH: 1'–1½' × 2' (30–45cm × 60cm)

LIGHT: full sun–partial shade

ZONES: 3–8

Siberian bugloss

If you love forget-me-nots, try this perennial charmer. It features loose sprays of tiny (¼ inch [6mm]), star-shaped, periwinkle flowers. They appear early, along with the spring bulbs and forsythia, and bloom with abandon for several weeks. The plant makes a wonderful "weaver" in areas where you've planted a variety of flowers, because the color goes with almost everything. An easy plant to grow, it does well in full sun and in shade—even dry shade. It will spread, but unwanted volunteers are easy to pull out.

Even if it didn't flower, Siberian bugloss would be a valuable addition to a lightly shaded garden as a groundcover because its heart-shaped leaves are attractive in their own right. They start out small, form a pretty carpet that disguises fading bulb foliage, and expand in size (sometimes to nearly 8 inches [20.5cm] across) as the summer goes by. Watch out for nibbling slugs, though, and set out bait if they start to disfigure the planting.

Campanula

Bellflower

BLOOM TIME: late spring–summer

HEIGHT/WIDTH: varies

LIGHT: full sun–partial shade

ZONES: 3–9 (most)

Bellflower

Campanula is a large genus, with all sorts of varieties, ranging in habit from stately border plants to rock garden specimens. Most are a cinch to grow, preferring full sun (light shade if your summers are especially hot) and decent soil that is neither too wet nor too dry. Slugs and snails adore them, however, so be prepared to do battle if these creatures are already present in your yard.

If you want a low-grower, try *C. carpatica*, which forms a mound 6 to 12 inches (15 to 30cm) tall. It covers itself in stalks of 1- to 2-inch (2.5 to 5cm) blue or white blooms for weeks in early summer to midsummer. And it can be per-

suaded to keep blooming if you deadhead regularly. It's a charmer in a pot, and fits in well in rock garden settings or the front of a flower border.

A taller choice, ideal for a starring role in your summer perennial border, is the peach-leaved bellflower, *C. persicifolia*. It grows up to 3½ feet (1m) tall, and displays its pretty, open-bell flowers (1½ to 2 inches [4 to 5cm] across) along the top half of its graceful stems. For a different effect, consider others whose flowers, still bell-shaped, appear in dense clusters, like the 2- to 5-foot (60 to 150cm) *C. lactiflora* or 1- to 3-foot (30 to 90cm) *C. glomerata*.

Catananche caerulea

Cupid's dart

BLOOM TIME: summer–early autumn

HEIGHT/WIDTH: 2' × 1' (60cm × 30cm)

LIGHT: full sun

ZONES: 4–9

Cupid's dart

A tough, charming plant, Cupid's dart forms neat, small clumps of grassy, gray-green foliage. It tosses up adorable little button buds (on long, wiry stems) that open to 2-inch (5cm) flowers of lilac-blue with a darker center. The flowers look a bit like those of their wild cousin chicory, and are a nice addition to summer bouquets. They dry as well as strawflowers, making them a favorite of flower arrangers and wreath-makers. For best drying results, harvest the flowers shortly after they open. The plant looks best massed, with all those small flowers and buds waving in unison in a summer breeze. Several color variations are available, among them var. *alba*, which has silvery white flowers, and 'Bicolor', which features white petals and a contrasting dark blue center.

Cupid's dart prefers soil on the dry side and tolerates drought. The plant's only real drawback is that it is seldom long-lived, though annual spring division helps. It also self-sows readily.

Centaurea montana

Mountain bluet, perennial cornflower

BLOOM TIME: early summer–early autumn

HEIGHT/WIDTH: 1'–2' × 2' (30–60cm × 60cm)

LIGHT: full sun–partial shade

ZONES: 3–8

Mountain bluet

There are other perennial cornflowers, but none with flowers quite as striking as these—they're an electric shade of dark blue, with a dark red eye in the center. About 2 to 3 inches (5 to 7.5cm) across, they have a loose, frilly look thanks to a relatively low petal count. Best of all, the plant blooms continually all summer, especially if you keep it well watered and deadheaded.

This plant grows about 2 feet (60cm) tall. It is well covered in dark green, lance-shaped foliage that provides a good contrasting stage for the remarkable flowers. It's not fussy about soil, and will spread rapidly to form robust colonies.

Like its wild relatives, mountain bluet has a generous, informal look that makes it a welcome addition to casual herb gardens or flower borders. Plant it with red-hued bee balms for a bold color duet, or aim for a softer look by pairing it with one of the lacy, silver-gray artemisias.

Centranthus ruber

Red valerian

BLOOM TIME: late spring–early autumn

HEIGHT/WIDTH: 1½'–3' × 1'–1½' (45–90cm × 30–45cm)

LIGHT: full sun–partial shade

ZONES: 4–8

Red valerian

Long popular in British and European gardens, this tough, agreeable valerian does splendidly in North America as well, sulking only in the South's hot, humid summers. The tiered flower stalks, up to 3 feet (90cm) tall, bear plenty of neat, lightly fragrant ½-inch (1.5cm) flowers in clusters. Usually they are raspberry or bright red, but white ones are also available and are easier to match with other perennials. All the varieties self-sow readily, and sometimes find homes in the most unlikely spots—between paving stones, or wedged into a rock wall.

The branching stems are sturdy and clothed in smooth, bluish green leaves. When the plant is given a prime spot in average-to-sandy soil, it looks terrific and may bloom for months, even all summer long. If it starts to become floppy, or if you'd like to induce a repeat bloom, it's safe to chop back the plant in the middle of the season—it will rebound.

Chrysanthemum

Garden mum

BLOOM TIME: autumn

HEIGHT/WIDTH: 1'–6' × 1½' (30cm–1.8m × 45cm)

LIGHT: full sun

ZONES: 4–9

'Cymbals' garden mum

Apparently the botanists have been hard at work on this group, shifting plants into new categories and assigning new botanical names. But gardeners and nurseries are paying little heed, and you'll still find your favorites (traditionally *C. × morifolium* or *C. × hortorum*) labeled as "mums."

If you've always just plunked a few red, yellow, or orange mums in your borders or flower boxes in the autumn perhaps it's time to take a fresh look at this group. The hybridizers have also been busy, and there are scads of exciting alternatives. Mums now come in a wide range of sizes, from little button blooms to robust 6-inch (15cm) flowers. As for color, you'll discover everything from rich, unfettered crimson to bicolors and tricolors that seem lit from within. You'll find these mainly in the mail-order catalogs (a couple specialize in a stunning array of mums; see Sources on page 119). You will probably be urged to order in the spring, so your plants can get a good start and give their best by the time autumn rolls around. Early planting also gives you the opportunity to pinch back the stems in midsummer to encourage the bushiest possible form.

Chrysogonum virginianum

Goldenstar, green-and-gold

BLOOM TIME: spring–autumn

HEIGHT/WIDTH: 4"–1' × 1' (10–30cm × 30cm)

LIGHT: full sun–partial shade

ZONES: 5–9

Goldenstar

For a shady spot that needs brightening, a little goldenstar is unbeatable. A low, spreading (but not invasive) ground-cover, it has rich green leaves and bears marvelous glowing yellow, 1½-inch (4cm) daisylike blooms on short stalks. If you grow it in soil that is neither boggy nor dry, it will bloom generously, perhaps even for the whole summer.

This plant is native to the Appalachians on south to Florida, and will surely thrive in gardens in that region. But it also does just fine further north, provided you give it a good winter mulch.

Mass plantings always look great and call attention to goldenstar's vivacious little flowers. Try massing it along a woodland walkway or bordering a line of shrubs. You can also successfully combine goldenstar with other perennials—plant it with native columbines, grape hyacinths, or even something taller, like Virginia bluebells.

Cimicifuga racemosa

Bugbane, black snakeroot

BLOOM TIME: midsummer

HEIGHT/WIDTH: 3'–6' × 3' (90cm–1.8m × 90cm)

LIGHT: full sun–partial shade

ZONES: 3–8

Bugbane

This is a tall, full plant, not for every garden, but spectacular in the right setting. It is best used in the back of a large border, where its imposing presence enhances rather than overwhelms. You might also place it in the middle of an island bed, where it can be admired from all sides.

Dark green, much-divided foliage creates a bushlike form up to about 3 feet (90cm) tall and wide. And the creamy white flower plumes, which rise an additional 2 to 3 feet (60 to 90cm) above the foliage, are quite a sight. The flowers are branched rather than in individual spires, so the effect is like a candelabra. They put on their regal show for several weeks in midsummer and never need propping up. Some nurseries don't mention the scent, while others tell you it's "rank," but the truth is that it's not very obtrusive.

Bugbane is long-lived and trouble-free, unfussy about soil, and asks only for sufficient moisture. In hot climates, or if you want extra drama from those remarkable flower plumes, grow it in partial shade.

Clematis hybrids

Clematis

BLOOM TIME: spring–early summer (some later)

HEIGHT/WIDTH: varies

LIGHT: full sun

ZONES: 3–9

'Nelly Moser' clematis

Clematis varieties may well be the most beautiful flowering vines in the world. This group includes many excellent old favorites, and worthy new varieties make their debut each season. You can plant them in the spring, but you may want to give them a head start by planting in the autumn. Your clematis won't appear to be doing much the first season but it is actually building its root system. In years to come, you will be delighted by its profuse flowering.

Hybrid clematis flowers come in nearly every color of the rainbow. They are big and broad, usually in the 4- to 9-inch (10 to 23cm) range, and often centered with a boss of yellow stamens (some are tipped with purple for even more

impact). The ever-dependable _C._ × _jackmanii_ is a heavy bloomer in royal purple from midsummer to autumn. 'Nelly Moser' is a late-spring bloomer that repeats in autumn. Its bicolor blooms of soft pink with a dark pink stripe in the center of each petal are as tempting as a peppermint stick. The double-flowered 'Duchess of Edinburgh' features fluffy white blooms in the summer.

Although hybrid clematis vines perform best in full sun, their roots need the cooling influence of a little shade and a few inches (centimeters) of mulch. So plant them at the bottom of a porch, tree, or shrub, or skirt their bases with shallow-rooted perennials or annuals.

Conradina verticillata

Cumberland rosemary

BLOOM TIME: late spring

HEIGHT/WIDTH: 15″ × 1′–2′ (38cm × 30–60cm)

LIGHT: full sun–partial shade

ZONES: 5–8

Cumberland rosemary

Unfortunately, we don't often see this plant in gardens. Its needled foliage looks very much like rosemary—but it is far hardier than rosemary. Tiny, pinkish mauve flowers cover the plant each spring. And it has a powerful fragrance, somewhere between mint and camphor. It would make a nice groundcover in a spot where you don't want to do any elaborate landscaping, or you could add it to a rock garden or plant it for ornamental effect in an herb garden.

Gardeners sometimes call it "rabbit bane" because rabbits seem never to nibble on it.

Native to a limited area in the Cumberland Mountains of eastern Kentucky and Tennessee, it has been listed as a federally protected plant. But nurseries have begun to propagate it and it is bound to grow in popularity as more gardeners discover its easygoing charms. Cumberland rosemary does best in lean, sandy soil—just like in the wild.

Coreopsis hybrids

Coreopsis

BLOOM TIME: summer

HEIGHT/WIDTH: 1'–3' × 2'–3' (30–90cm × 60–90cm)

LIGHT: full sun

ZONES: 5–9

'Moonbeam' threadleaf coreopsis

This genus contains some of the finest, toughest perennial border plants going, and no sunny garden should be without a few. All bloom generously over a long period, do well in a wide range of soils, adapt easily to drought once established, and combine nicely with other flowers. The daisylike blossoms are usually yellow.

Among the best cultivars are those derived from *C. grandiflora*. The widely available and deservedly popular 'Sunray' has very full-petaled, bright yellow double flowers on 18- to 24-inch (45 to 60cm) plants. 'Early Sunrise' also

bears double yellow flowers in incredible profusion, and is about the same height, but has a more compact habit.

The threadleaf coreopsis, *C. verticillata*, includes several worthwhile cultivars. Perhaps the best of these is the 2-foot (60cm) 'Moonbeam', which billows with lovely pale yellow flowers. The thin, needlelike leaves and graceful stalks give the plant an airy quality. It makes an excellent addition to perennial borders, where it flatters rather than overpowers its companions. Try it with blue campanulas, verbenas, or lavenders.

Crambe cordifolia

Colewort

BLOOM TIME: late spring–early summer

HEIGHT/WIDTH: 4′–7′ × 3′ (1.2–2.1m ×90cm)

LIGHT: full sun

ZONES: 6–9

Colewort

A tall, striking plant, colewort is easy to grow and always excites comments from garden visitors. It does need full sun to do its best, and the soil should be more alkaline than acid, making it a better choice for gardens of the Northwest and the prairie states and provinces. It forms a substantial mound of broad, cabbagelike leaves (up to 2 feet [60cm] across!) that remain dark green all season. In early summer, it sends up stout, multibranched stalks, to an imposing height of 5 feet (1.5m). These are laden with clouds of tiny white blooms that look very much like baby's breath. You may have to provide stake support.

Colewort asks little of the gardener in exchange for this magnificent show, except adequate water to support the massive leaves. You'll also want to give it an open spot where it can live up to its full, dramatic potential.

Crocosmia

Montebretia

BLOOM TIME: mid–late summer

HEIGHT/WIDTH: 1½'–3' × 1' (45–90cm × 30cm)

LIGHT: full sun

ZONES: 5–9

'Lucifer' montebretia

This is not a plant for the fainthearted. The sprays of tubular flowers, borne along arching stalks, are a fiery shade of reddish orange and bloom for weeks at a time. The most widely available cultivar, 'Lucifer', has brilliant scarlet flowers. All make for splendid bouquets. In the garden and in the vase, the best companions for montebretia are other hot-colored bloomers—try it with any yellow or orange daisylike flower.

A clump-former, it grows from small corms similar to those of gladiolus. But montebretia is hardier and you need not dig up the corms for the winter unless you live north of Zone 5. The foliage is dark green and swordlike, and blends well in the garden when the plant is not in bloom. In order to thrive, this plant needs moist soil. If you are concerned that the soil will dry out between waterings, lay down a mulch. In the South, give it some shade.

Delphinium hybrids

Delphinium, larkspur

BLOOM TIME: spring–summer

HEIGHT/WIDTH: 3′–8′ × 2′–3′ (90cm–2.4m × 60–90cm)

LIGHT: full sun

ZONES: 3–9

Delphinium

A foolproof delphinium? Can such a thing exist? If you're intimidated by these beauties, or have been disappointed in the past, vow first and foremost to give them the best conditions you can. You will be richly rewarded.

It's true that the magnificent flower stalks are prone to toppling or breaking in strong breezes or summer rain showers. Staking the stalks early is always wise, but you should also be sure to plant your delphiniums in a protected spot. A fence, wall, porch, or hedge can all act as buffers.

The soil should be rich in organic matter, and you ought to fertilize them monthly—delphiniums are greedy feeders.

Arguably the best of the delphiniums are the widely available *D. × elatum* hybrids, which have dense, full spikes of flowers. These come in an extensive range of colors—white, near pink, lavender, purple, and many variations on blue, often with contrasting "bees" in the centers. The Blackmore & Langdon series is of superior quality, as are the Pacific hybrids.

Dianthus

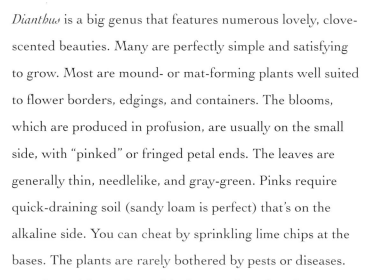

Pinks

BLOOM TIME: varies depending on species

HEIGHT/WIDTH: 6″–1½′ × 8″–12″ (15–45cm × 20.5–30cm)

LIGHT: full sun

ZONES: 4 or 5–10

Maiden pinks

Dianthus is a big genus that features numerous lovely, clove-scented beauties. Many are perfectly simple and satisfying to grow. Most are mound- or mat-forming plants well suited to flower borders, edgings, and containers. The blooms, which are produced in profusion, are usually on the small side, with "pinked" or fringed petal ends. The leaves are generally thin, needlelike, and gray-green. Pinks require quick-draining soil (sandy loam is perfect) that's on the alkaline side. You can cheat by sprinkling lime chips at the bases. The plants are rarely bothered by pests or diseases.

The maiden pink (*D. deltoides*) is a drought-tolerant mat-former that grows to between 6 and 12 inches (15 and 30cm) high. The small, ⅞-inch (2cm) flowers come in pink, rose, red, and white. Cheddar pink (*D. gratianopolitanus*), at 9 to 12 inches (23 to 30cm) high, forms neat, dense mounds from which emerge wiry stems that bear small, solitary flowers about ½ inch (1.5) across, usually in pink, sometimes in red. 'Bath's Pink' wins raves for its old-fashioned beauty and spicy fragrance. It is especially beloved by Southerners, who prize its ability to weather their hot, humid summers. The cottage pink (*D. plumarius*) is a larger, hummock-forming plant (up to 2 feet [60cm] tall) whose long-blooming 1-inch (2.5cm) flowers are often found in fluffy, double hybrids of white, pink, and red.

Dicentra spectabilis

Bleeding-heart

BLOOM TIME: spring

HEIGHT/WIDTH: $2'–3' \times 2'$ (60–90cm $\times$ 60cm)

LIGHT: partial–full shade

ZONES: 3–9

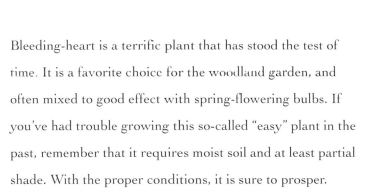

Bleeding-heart

Bleeding-heart is a terrific plant that has stood the test of time. It is a favorite choice for the woodland garden, and often mixed to good effect with spring-flowering bulbs. If you've had trouble growing this so-called "easy" plant in the past, remember that it requires moist soil and at least partial shade. With the proper conditions, it is sure to prosper.

Bleeding-heart's ferny, much-divided foliage forms a beautiful, loose mound about as wide as it is tall. The endearing 1-inch (2.5cm) locket-shaped flowers line lovely arching stems. The plain species is pink-and-white flowered. A cultivar, 'Alba', is all white, and not quite as vigorous a grower. Both will stay in bloom for up to six weeks, provided that your spring weather is not too capricious. After the flowers are finished blooming, the attractive foliage remains and holds its own fairly well for the rest of the season. In warmer areas or drier soils, however, the plant may simply throw in the towel and go dormant by midsummer.

Digitalis

Foxglove

BLOOM TIME: early–midsummer

HEIGHT/WIDTH: 3′–5′ × 2′ (90cm–1.5m × 60cm)

LIGHT: full sun–partial shade

ZONES: 4–7 (most)

Foxglove

Foxgloves have been cherished by generations of gardeners because they are so handsome and so low-maintenance. Most are short-lived, and are better considered biennials—which simply means that they generally delay bloom until their second season. But if you grow them in moist, fertile soil, you'll always have them, for they self-sow with abandon. There are many enchanting cultivars and mixes from which to choose. But you'll notice that the self-sown seedlings of later years have their own ideas about what color to be, due to rather complex foxglove genetics. So fox-

gloves are not for color purists, but rather for gardeners who enjoy exuberant variability.

The old-fashioned *D. purpurea* is 2 to 5 feet (60cm to 1.5m) tall and comes in purple as well as pastel shades of pink, mauve, yellow, and white. 'Alba', an all-white variety, is a real stunner, especially when grown in partial shade with dark green foliage as a backdrop. Shade gardeners who want a break from white flowers will appreciate the chiffon yellow bells of *D. ambigua* (also known as *D. grandiflora*), borne on stalks that are 2 to 3 feet (60 to 90cm) tall.

Doronicum orientale

Leopard's-bane

BLOOM TIME: spring–early summer

HEIGHT/WIDTH: 1½'–2' × 1'–1½' (45–60cm × 30–45cm)

LIGHT: full sun–partial shade

ZONES: 3–8

Leopard's-bane

Unlike most yellow daisies, leopard's-bane blooms in spring, which suggests a whole different range of plant combinations. Its cheerful, butter yellow blooms (1 to 2 inches [2.5 to 5cm] across), produced in profusion and held up proudly, look terrific in the company of bold red tulips, for instance, or the blue flowers of brunnera. The plant is neither tall nor sprawling, which is a plus when you have specific plans for it. Its leaves are dark green, heart-shaped, and toothed.

They grow thickly at the base and line the stems but stay short of the flowers. This plant tends to go dormant in the summer, particularly where summers are hot.

Grow leopard's-bane in sun or shade, but make sure the soil is on the moist side. Mulching helps; otherwise, this energetic plant will ask little and give much.

Echinacea purpurea

Purple coneflower

BLOOM TIME: summer

HEIGHT/WIDTH: 2′–4′ × 1½′–2′ (60–120cm × 45–60cm)

LIGHT: full sun

ZONES: 3–8

Purple coneflower

Perhaps the most dramatic of the daisylike perennials, purple coneflower has big, splendid blooms. The petals are long, up to 2 ½ inches (6.5cm), and are generally light purple. The orange-to-bronze cone in the center is symmetrical and very prominent. Often the petals droop downward from the cone, giving the plants a whimsical, shuttlecock appearance and providing a welcoming stage for visiting butterflies. Carried in great numbers on a coarse, well-branched plant, these blooms make for wonderful bouquets. Flower arrangers love to collect and dry them for the central cones alone—though if you leave them be, the plant will often self-sow and add to your display with each passing year.

A native of the prairies, this stalwart plant loves full sun and is content with average, not overly rich, soil. It has a hefty root system, and develops a deep taproot, so moving and dividing is not recommended. However, this means it will weather periods of drought well and contribute many years of beauty to your garden.

Echinops ritro

Globe thistle

BLOOM TIME: summer

HEIGHT/WIDTH: 2'–4' × 1½' (60–120cm × 45cm)

LIGHT: full sun

ZONES: 3–8

Globe thistle

Ordinarily, thistles are considered weeds, but not this lavender-blue beauty. The 1- to 2-inch (2.5 to 5cm) globe-shaped flower heads are actually composed of many tiny florets, and are attractive viewed from any angle. There are a couple of nice cultivars in different shades. Look for 'Taplow Blue', which is more silvery blue or steel blue, and 'Veitch's Blue', a darker blue. Globe thistle makes a wonderful color contribution to perennial borders—and is especially terrific in the company of yellow daisies or daylilies. If you wish to cut some to dry, do so before the blooms have opened or they'll shatter.

The plants themselves are admittedly a bit rough. The leaves are dark green and bristly, with spiny tips. But the prickles are not as dangerous as those on some wild thistles. Over the course of a summer, the lower leaves may dry up and fall off, so plant globe thistle well back in the border where this tendency won't be exposed.

Epimedium × rubrum

Epimedium

BLOOM TIME: spring

HEIGHT/WIDTH: 6"–1' × 1'–1½' (15–30cm × 30–45cm)

LIGHT: partial–full shade

ZONES: 4–8

Epimedium

If you find the ubiquitous pachysandra boring or too bold as a groundcover, you might try the delicate-looking but naturally tough epimedium instead. Its preference is for damp shade, but it will also do well in traditionally difficult settings, such as under a tree or in a dry shade area. Epimedium is not a fast increaser, so you should plant individuals fairly close together—approximately 1 foot (30cm) apart.

Like all epimediums, this species has pretty, oblong heart–shaped leaflets on wiry stems. The leaves are red when they emerge in early spring, and change to red-tinged green over the course of the summer. They are not evergreen over the winter. The spurred flowers appear for a brief but generous display in spring. They are about 1 inch (2.5cm) across and bright pink to almost crimson, sometimes flushed with yellow.

Eupatorium purpureum

Joe-Pye weed

BLOOM TIME: summer–early autumn

HEIGHT/WIDTH: 4'–6' × 2'–4' (1.2–1.8m × 60–120cm)

LIGHT: full sun–partial shade

ZONES: 4–8

'Gateway' Joe-Pye weed

Big and imposing, Joe-Pye weed is best planted in groups at the back of the border. It is sure to dazzle visitors to your garden and draw butterflies like a magnet. The strong, erect but hollow stems are wine red and tall, and are clothed in handsome, toothed leaves that may grow as long as 1 foot (30cm). Flowers don't appear until later in the summer, but they're worth the wait. They foam forth in clusters of rose pink to light purple, and have a sweet, enticing fragrance.

A native North American plant, Joe-Pye weed is tough and hardy. Its only preference seems to be for damp soil. Otherwise, it needs little attention to maintain its spectacular form and annual performance.

Other types of Joe-Pye weed come in different sizes and colors. The most widely available cultivar is probably 'Gateway'. This handsome hybrid between *E. purpureum* and *E. maculatum* features darker, reddish purple blooms.

Euphorbia

Spurge

BLOOM TIME: spring–early summer

HEIGHT/WIDTH: varies

LIGHT: full sun–partial shade

ZONES: varies

'Wulfenii' spurge

Euphorbia is an intriguing and enduringly popular genus of diverse plants. The plants have long, thin leaves, dense along their stems, and unusual "flowers" that are really colored bracts. You will find that they are trouble-free where the summers are not too hot or humid. Insects and diseases are not a problem, and the plants grow well in many soils (if you avoid clay and waterlogged areas). Do place them where you want them to stay, because they develop substantial taproots.

The popular *E. characias* is dramatic and tall, growing to 4 feet (1.2m). It has big, chartreuse, nearly globe-shaped flower heads. These contrast dramatically with the blue green leaves. *E. griffithii* 'Fireglow' is also widely grown, and is valued for its orange-red bracts and red-veined leaves. It reaches 2 to 3 feet (60 to 90cm) tall. Both are noble contributions to a perennial border, or can be used for impressive mass or bank plantings. *E. polychroma* (also known as *E. epithymoides*) is a stout smaller plant, growing in mounds of 1 to 2 feet (30 to 60cm). It owes its name to the fact that it displays different colors in different seasons: citrus yellow flowers in spring, lime green foliage by summer, and russet or red leaves in autumn. Beware of the sap of all these plants; some people have found it causes skin irritation.

Filipendula rubra

Queen-of-the-prairie

BLOOM TIME: summer

HEIGHT/WIDTH: 6'–8' × 3'–4' (1.8–2.4m × 90–120cm)

LIGHT: full sun–partial shade

ZONES: 3–9

Queen-of-the-prairie

Queen-of-the-prairie is a towering, bushy beauty. Its elegant flower plumes resemble those of the shrub spirea, but these are longer—up to 9 inches (23cm) in length. The plumes are composed of myriad tiny pink flowers. For a deeper pink-rose show, try the cultivar 'Venusta'. You'll find that deadheading prolongs the already generous bloom period. The flowers are joined by jagged forest green leaves that cover the especially strong stems. This plant stands up well to wind and weather.

Queen-of-the-prairie is not a dryland plant, despite what the name suggests. It requires damp or even wet soil, so it might be just right for a boggy spot along a back stone wall or fence. Some water gardeners border the far side of their pools with it—with spectacular results.

When well-situated, queen-of-the-prairie will grow exuberantly and spread by means of runners. So unless you've planted it in a slightly wild spot, you may have to intervene to control it.

Gaillardia × grandiflora

Blanket flower

BLOOM TIME: summer

HEIGHT/WIDTH: 2'–3' × 1'–2' (60–90cm × 30–60cm)

LIGHT: full sun

ZONES: 3–9

'Goblin' blanket flower

Big, cheerful, daisylike flowers cover this sturdy plant for most of the summer. Up to 4 inches (10cm) across, their rosy red or orange-red petals are tipped with bright yellow; the centers are broad and usually in a complementary shade of bronze or orange. The best cultivar is 'Goblin', a dwarf plant that grows only 1 foot (30cm) tall and is constantly covered with vibrant red-and-yellow blooms. The well-named 'Burgundy' is worth seeking out if you want a solid-colored flower.

The plant forms tidy clumps of handsome, somewhat fuzzy foliage. Blanket flower is undemanding, thriving easily in poor soil, drought conditions, and long, hot summers. A natural for low-maintenance flower borders, this sunny beauty looks terrific in the company of other primary-color flowers such as yellow coreopsis, red salvia, and blue veronica.

Galium
odoratum

Sweet woodruff

BLOOM TIME: spring

HEIGHT/WIDTH: 6″–1′ × 1′ (15–30cm × 30cm)

LIGHT: partial–full shade

ZONES: 3–9

Sweet woodruff

It's hard to imagine a prettier groundcover for shade. The long, thin, apple green leaves occur in whorls, and spread slowly but surely over the years to densely cover large areas. When they are joined by the tiny, dainty, white- to cream-colored flowers (only ¼ inch [6mm] across), the effect is downright enchanting. The name refers to the fact that both leaves and flowers exude a sweet, spicy scent when dried. Some craftspeople like to add sweet woodruff to the stuffing in pillows and mattresses, and it has also been used to enhance homemade wine.

Plant this charmer on banks, along walkways, under trees, or even in the gaps between walkway stones. It will grow in damp or dry soil alike, and is very durable. "Volunteers" that appear beyond their bounds are easily pulled out.

Gaura lindheimeri

White gaura

BLOOM TIME: summer

HEIGHT/WIDTH: 3′–4′ × 1′–2′ (90–120cm × 30–60cm)

LIGHT: full sun

ZONES: 5–9

White gaura

It's surprising that this extremely tough and exuberant plant isn't grown more widely. All summer long, it's a fountain of lovely, delicate-looking white flowers that age to a pretty shade of light rosy pink. These are carried on the upper part of long, willowy stems. The leaves, which are dark to medium green and spear-shaped, tend to remain low on the plant and don't steal the show.

To give its best, gaura deserves a place out in the open or a spot in the perennial border with ample elbow room.

Established plants have a sturdy, fleshy root (like a carrot) and are quite drought-tolerant, but well-drained soil is still an important requirement. Gardeners in the hot, humid South are especially enthusiastic about this lovely plant, as it thrives in scorching sun, enervating heat, and poor soil. It also does well up North, but may not grow as large and may not bloom until later in the summer in cooler areas. It falters in the shade, so make sure to give it a site in full sun.

Geranium

Cranesbill, hardy geranium

BLOOM TIME: varies

HEIGHT/WIDTH: 1'–2' × 1'–2' (30–60cm × 30–60cm)

LIGHT: full sun–partial shade

ZONES: 5–9

'Wargrave Pink' and 'Johnson's Blue' cranesbills

Hardy geraniums are sprawlers or mound-formers that cover themselves with pretty saucer-shaped flowers. These come in a range of colors from white to pink to blue, and the dainty petals often have darker-colored veining. The attractive leaves are usually palm-shaped and deeply lobed or cut. They may turn red in autumn, adding a nice late splash of color. The cranesbills are a versatile, easygoing addition to any flower border. They thrive in good, but not overly rich soil and benefit from some shade in the heat of the day.

Probably the finest and, not surprisingly, the most widely planted cranesbill is a hybrid named 'Johnson's Blue'. It produces loads of wonderful, true-blue 2-inch (5cm) flowers. The plant sprawls, so let it act as a "weaver" among other plants. Another choice selection is the lovely and vigorous *G. endressi* 'Wargrave Pink'; the 1-inch (2.5cm) blooms are bright pink. *G. sanguineum* 'Album' has pure white 1½ -inch (4cm) flowers against a backdrop of dark green leaves.

Gypsophila paniculata

Baby's-breath

BLOOM TIME: summer

HEIGHT/WIDTH: 1½'–4' × 3'–4' (45–120cm × 90–120cm)

LIGHT: full sun

ZONES: 3–9

Baby's-breath

It's easy to grow your own baby's-breath. And this plant blooms so generously that you'll have a sweet, airy addition to your garden plus plenty of opportunities to harvest sprays for bouquets. There are many cultivars to choose from beyond the familiar white species. The double-flowered ones are especially desirable—the flowers are a little bigger and a bit fluffier. Look for 'Bristol Fairy' (white) and 'Pink Fairy'. They make nice fillers for sunny parts of the yard.

They billow right over fading bulb foliage and other spring bloomers, and make spiky-flowered plants look less stiff. It's fine to cut flowers for drying even when the plant is in full bloom.

Baby's-breath will do best in soil that is neutral to slightly alkaline, fertile, and moist. The bushes can get a tangled, unkempt look unless you offer support in the form of stakes and string early in the season.

Helenium autumnale

Sneezeweed

BLOOM TIME: late summer

HEIGHT/WIDTH: $4' \times 1'–2'$ (120cm × 30–60cm)

LIGHT: full sun

ZONES: 3–9

Sneezeweed

A perky late-season bloomer, this clump-forming plant began as a pretty wildflower and is now available in a wide range of cultivated varieties. (The common name is a misnomer, perhaps acquired because it blooms at the same time as the real culprit, ragweed.) All of the cultivars are as hardy and eager to bloom as their parent. The branched stems bear loads of 2-inch (5cm) daisylike flowers. The centers are often darker than the notched petals, which droop slightly. 'Moerheim Beauty' has bronze-red flowers that age to burnt orange. The aptly named 'Brilliant' has rich orange flowers with a darker center. A hybrid called 'Kugelsonne' has sunny yellow blooms and a chartreuse center. Try combining some of these with the various autumn-blooming asters for a spirited display.

Give sneezeweed moist soil for best results. In any case, it tends to get rangy, so some gardeners cut it back to about a foot (30cm) high in midsummer. It will bloom about six to eight weeks later.

Helianthus × multiflorus

Perennial sunflower

BLOOM TIME: summer

HEIGHT/WIDTH: 4'–6' × 2' (1.2–1.8m × 60cm)

LIGHT: full sun

ZONES: 3–9

'Flore Pleno' perennial sunflower

These hybrid sunflowers are derived from the familiar annuals, and share with their relatives an enthusiasm for growing tall and wide. But these are perennial, of course, and the flowers are substantially smaller—generally between 3 and 5 inches (7.5 and 13cm) across. They are usually a sunny yellow color. A number of the cultivated varieties are double, and some (notably 'Flore Pleno' and 'Loddon Gold') contain so many petals that the blossoms look almost like those of chrysanthemums.

You can expect loads of these bright flowers starting in midsummer and continuing well into autumn. The plant may need staking. It is probably best situated toward the back of your display where its size and exuberance won't overwhelm its neighbors. Such a setting will also downplay the coarse foliage. Despite these seeming drawbacks, sunflowers are hard to beat for dependable, late-season splendor.

Helleborus orientalis

Lenten rose

BLOOM TIME: early spring

HEIGHT/WIDTH: $2' \times 2'$ (60cm × 60cm)

LIGHT: partial–full shade

ZONES: 4–8

'Atropurpureus' Lenten rose

Easier to grow than its cousin the Christmas rose (*H. niger*), just as gorgeous, and somewhat larger-flowered, this hellebore is often among the first signs of spring. The nodding flowers are slightly cup-shaped, 3 to 4 inches (7.5 to 10cm) across, and come in shades of cream, pink, rose, lavender, or purple, often blushed or speckled with a darker hue. At first glance, they are reminiscent of old-fashioned, single-form roses. The leaves are carried in compound leaflets, and may be evergreen if your winters are not too harsh.

Named cultivars are hard to come by, but you might try some seed-grown hellebores in a shady spot and wait to see what comes up. To ensure a great performance, pamper them with cool, moist, and slightly alkaline soil. Beware: both leaves and roots are poisonous.

Hemerocallis

Daylily

BLOOM TIME: summer

HEIGHT/WIDTH: varies

LIGHT: full sun–partial shade

ZONES: 3–9

Daylily

Where would the perennial garden be without daylilies? They are so dependable, so long blooming, and so handsome, that few plants are their equals. There are literally hundreds of named varieties available, so don't settle for plain old yellow or orange if you want something more exciting. Order a catalog from a specialist (see page 119), and feast your eyes on the amazing range of choices. Some newer, sunfast reds are actually a glorious crimson, and there are countless worthy bicolors (how about a peach-colored daylily with a lavender throat?). For a stouter plant and a fuller flower, consider one of the "tetraploid" hybrids.

Daylilies will grow in many settings and soils, and will be utterly spectacular if you don't take them for granted. Grow them in fertile soil that is adequately drained. Water deeply when the weather is dry and remove spent blossoms regularly—they owe their name to the fact that individual blossoms really do only last one day.

Heuchera × brizoides

Coralbells

BLOOM TIME: spring–summer

HEIGHT/WIDTH: 1'–2½' ×1' (30–75cm × 30cm)

LIGHT: full sun–partial shade

ZONES: 3–9

'Bressingham Hybrids' coralbells

Coralbells are often treasured for their foliage. The leaves, generally green, are produced in mannerly clumps, and look a bit like those of ivy, though more rounded. They remain attractive all season long, making the plant an ideal choice for a semishady perennial border or even a groundcover. *H. × brizoides* hybrids, however, are also treasured for their petite but splendid flowers. Arrayed along tall, graceful stalks above the leaves, these remain in bloom for several weeks in spring or early summer. 'Mt. St. Helens' has red flowers, 'Coral Cloud' has pinkish coral flowers, and 'June Bride' and 'White Cloud' have white flowers. When planted in groups, coralbells in bloom bring an enchanting, fairy-land quality to the garden. Relatives and parents of *H. × brizoides* offer an expanded range of leaf colors. The renowned 'Palace Purple' sports rich leaves ranging from maroon to royal purple. Other selections are bronze, russet, or silvery, or feature these colors on their veins for a rich, tapestrylike appearance.

Hibiscus moscheutos

Rose mallow

BLOOM TIME: summer

HEIGHT/WIDTH: 4'–6' × 3' (1.2–1.8m × 90cm)

LIGHT: full sun

ZONES: 5–9

Rose mallow

This perennial produces flowers of amazing size—up to 10 inches (25.5cm) across! They're in the classic hibiscus form, complete with five broad, silky petals and that distinctive bottlebrushlike center part. These appear in profusion for weeks on end in the latter part of the summer. You'll find rose mallow offered in red, pink, and white. Unless you have the space and are willing to let several plants steal the scene, your best bet is to tuck just a plant or two into a border with other bold performers.

The plant itself grows quickly, especially in organically rich soil, which it relishes. It is large enough to be mistaken for a shrub, and has strong stems that stand up well to wind, rarely requiring staking. The soft lime green foliage is attractive but vulnerable to Japanese beetles. As with other hibiscus, the rose mallow is also susceptible to white fly. Try to keep the plant healthy, and spray with insecticidal soap if need be.

Hosta

Hosta, plantain lily

BLOOM TIME: varies

HEIGHT/WIDTH: varies

LIGHT: partial–full shade

ZONES: 3–9

'Golden Tiara' hosta

Hostas are popular because they are so simple to grow and bring a cool beauty to shady spots. The trick is to choose wisely from among the many selections. Consider size first: there are small mounding types that stay under 12 inches (30.5cm) across, as well as great broad-shouldered ones that spread out at maturity to 2 ½ feet (75cm) across. There is also great diversity in leaf color, perhaps more so than with any other foliage plant. Hostas range from soft blue-green to shiny, minty bright green. Many varieties are white- or gold-rimmed or feature light green or creamy variegation. And last but not least, there is texture—some hosta leaves are almost smooth, some are ribbed, and some are quite puckered. All this variety means irresistible opportunities for dressing up your shade garden, whether you plant masses under the high trees or use only a few as accent plants. Although its greatest value is as a foliage plant, don't overlook hosta flowers, which come in either white or various shades of lavender. The blooms line arching stalks and appear anywhere from late spring to late summer, depending on the variety. They can be quite a show in their own right, especially if you've planted a grouping.

Iberis sempervirens

Candytuft

BLOOM TIME: late spring

HEIGHT/WIDTH: 6″–1′ × 2′ (15–30cm × 60cm)

LIGHT: full sun–partial shade

ZONES: 3–9

Candytuft

Why plant the same old annual white alyssum as an edging or in a rock garden when you can get bigger, brighter flowers on a perennial plant? Candytuft has much to recommend it: the plant forms tidy mounds or mats of thin, glossy leaves that look good before, during, and after blooming. And the 1- to 2-inch (1.2 to 2.5cm) flowers are fabulous. Carried in dense, lacy clusters, they literally cover the plant every spring. A popular variety, 'Snowflake', has slightly larger flower heads and stays around 10 inches (25.5cm) tall. 'Little Gem' is a perky dwarf edition.

This plant adores full sun, and needs well-drained soil. It's a good idea after flowering to chop back the plants a few inches (centimeters) to maintain their compact form. For a spectacular, low-maintenance display, try underplanting a maroon-leaved weeping Japanese maple with a skirt of candytuft—it'll stop traffic.

Iris spp.

Tall bearded irises

BLOOM TIME: late spring

HEIGHT/WIDTH: generally 3'–4' × 2'–3' (90–120cm × 60–90cm)

LIGHT: full sun

ZONES: 4–9

Tall bearded iris

There are few sights as splendid as a stand of blooming tall bearded irises, backlit by the sun. They come in practically every color of the rainbow, including bicolors. Some are sweetly fragrant. Check out the newer introductions, and watch the nurseries for special deals on large quantities, because mass plantings are truly an unrivaled spectacle. Unfortunately, these flowers do not bloom for very long, but gardeners continue to lose their hearts to them, anyway.

The secrets to growing terrific bearded irises are simple. They need well-drained soil so their rhizomes don't rot or succumb to disease. Never bury the rhizomes completely; they should be planted only halfway into the ground.

Always keep your irises groomed, both of spent leaves and passed flowers. Also, clean up the ground around your planting so diseases and pests are not harbored in dead leaves or other garden debris. Don't mulch. Tall bearded irises are vulnerable to the dreaded iris borer. If you catch borers before the rhizomes become hollow shells, remove and discard all affected plants and check the surrounding soil. Don't spare the life of a single fat pink grub.

Iris sibirica

Siberian iris

BLOOM TIME: early summer

HEIGHT/WIDTH: 2′–4′ × 2′–3′ (60–120cm × 60–90cm)

LIGHT: full sun–partial shade

ZONES: 4–9

Siberian iris

There are many excellent reasons why Siberian irises are so prized by perennial gardeners. Flocks of pretty 2- to 3-inch (5 to 7.5cm) flowers appear dependably year after year. And after the irises are finished blooming, the neat clumps of straplike green foliage remain an attractive contribution to the flower border. Siberian irises grow well in most areas and most soils, and they are hardly ever prey to any pests or diseases.

Traditionally blue, purple, or white, these tough irises have received attention from hybridizers, and the result is many lovely variations on those colors. 'Ewen' has wine red flowers; 'Summer Sky' has soft, sky blue blooms; and 'Orville Fay' has delphinium blue flowers with darker veining. The whimsically named 'Butter and Eggs' is a white-and-yellow bicolor. If you shop around, you'll find dozens of other tempting choices.

Kniphofia uvaria

Red-hot-poker, torch lily

BLOOM TIME: late summer–early autumn

HEIGHT/WIDTH: 2½'–3½' (75–105cm) × 1½'–2'
(45–60cm)

LIGHT: full sun

ZONES: 6–9

Red-hot-poker

These brilliantly colored bloomers are a wonderful contribution to the late-season garden. For most of the summer, the tufts of ordinary-looking grassy leaves (usually blue-green in color), call little attention to themselves. Then the flower spikes emerge and rise a foot (30cm) or more into the air. They bear tapering spires of 1- to 2-inch (2.5 to 5cm) drooping, tubular flowers; these take on a bicolor look because the lower flowers (which open first) are one color, and the upper ones another color. The species is yellow below and fiery orange above. Plant them in a row, along a wall or fence, for example, if you want a real showstopper.

Most red-hot-pokers these days are actually hybrids. Many are in the yellow-orange-red range, but some are solid colors that are a little easier to combine with other flowers. Among these, you'll find the aptly named 'Vanilla', and the similar 'Little Maid' (whose creamy white spikes are especially long). Gold and yellow ones are also pleasant choices; look for 'Ada' and 'Primrose Beauty'.

Lamium maculatum

Lamium

BLOOM TIME: summer

HEIGHT/WIDTH: $1'$–$1\frac{1}{2}' \times 1'$ (30–45cm $\times$ 30cm)

LIGHT: partial–full shade

ZONES: 4–8

'White Nancy' lamium

An easygoing, creeping groundcover for shade, lamium offers unique, variegated foliage. The oval leaves are a fresh green, spotted, ribbed, or marked with white, light green, or silver. 'White Nancy' and 'Beacon Silver', the most commonly seen cultivars, have green-rimmed foliage that is otherwise entirely silver.

A nice plus about these plants is their flowers, which nearly steal the show when they appear for several weeks each summer. They're only $\frac{1}{2}$ to 1 inch (1.2 to 2.5cm) long, and have a hooded shape. But they're borne in tight little clusters that stand slightly above the foliage. 'White Nancy' has white flowers, which combine with the leaves to make the plants "pop" out of the shade. 'Beacon Silver' has pretty pink flowers.

Essentially a trouble-free plant, lamium will obligingly carpet great areas, even in deep shade. Moist, well-drained soil is best, but the plant will manage even without perfect conditions.

Leucanthemum × superbum

Shasta daisy

BLOOM TIME: summer

HEIGHT/WIDTH: 1'–3' × 2' (30–90cm × 60cm)

LIGHT: full sun–partial shade

ZONES: 5–9

'Little Princess' Shasta daisy

This classic daisy is an old favorite. The large flowers (up to 5 inches [13cm] across) are a crisp white centered with sunny yellow. They cover a somewhat rounded bush of strong stems, loosely lined with skinny, toothed leaves. Don't hesitate to pick plenty of bouquets—it will inspire the plant to continue pumping out blooms all summer long.

You'll discover a number of worthwhile cultivated varieties, including many with double or semidouble flowers. For smaller gardens or tighter spots, consider growing a more compact selection, such as 'Little Princess' or 'Little Miss Muffet'. A newer variety named 'Becky' is bushier and leafier than its parent, blooms a little later, and has been winning raves from Southern gardeners for its ability to endure heat and humidity.

Generally speaking, Shasta daisy is no trouble to grow. But it does need well-drained, fertile soil. If the plant sits in a puddle all winter, it may falter or even die. Also, it performs best in cooler summers, so if yours are hot and steamy, offer Shasta daisy some afternoon shade and keep it well watered.

Liatris spicata

Spike gayfeather

BLOOM TIME: summer

HEIGHT/WIDTH: 2'–5' × 1½' (60cm–1.5m × 45cm)

LIGHT: full sun

ZONES: 3–9

Spike gayfeather

Treasured by bouquet lovers, spike gayfeather is a champ. It blooms eagerly and handsomely, bearing wonderful, dense spires of small purple flowers. These are carried one to a stem, making harvesting easy. They last a long time in a vase and dry beautifully, too. If you can hold back from picking them, however, your garden will soon be hosting lots of butterflies.

A native of the American prairies, spike gayfeather is a tough plant. It does best in somewhat sandy, fertile soil, and develops a strong tuberous rootstock that stores water for survival during dry spells.

A number of terrific cultivars have been developed from the species. The popular 'Kobold' is shorter, around 2 feet (60cm) tall, and has dark reddish purple blooms. (Try it alongside a yellow flower, such as coreopsis, for a striking combination.) 'Floristan White' has gorgeous, pure white spikes.

Linum perenne

Blue flax

BLOOM TIME: late spring–summer

HEIGHT/WIDTH: 1′–2′ × 1′–2′ (30–60cm × 30–60cm)

LIGHT: full sun

ZONES: 5–9

Blue flax

A must for casual cottage garden planting schemes, this lovely blue flower has many endearing qualities. The slim, arching stems bear clouds of sweet, almost delicate 1- to 2-inch (2.5 to 5cm) blooms over a long period. They need sun to open. On hot days, they drop their petals by midafternoon–but the flowers are replaced the next day.

The plant has an appealing, vaselike profile. It sports very thin—almost wispy—foliage in a complementary shade of bluish green. You'll find it easy to slip blue flax into perennial borders. It looks lovely in the neighborhood of many different plants, from pale yellow 'Moonbeam' coreopsis to pink roses.

Blue flax is not long-lived, even when grown in the well-drained, sandy soil it prefers. But it always self-sows, so you'll never be without it.

Liriope muscari

Lilyturf

BLOOM TIME: late summer–autumn

HEIGHT/WIDTH: 1′–2′ × 1½′ (30–60cm × 45cm)

LIGHT: partial–full shade

ZONES: 6–10

'Variegatum' lilyturf

Lilyturf is a staple in areas with long, hot, and steamy summers. It is one of the few edging or groundcover plants that maintains a cool freshness in those conditions. The spiky leaves are grasslike and narrow, but still substantial. A naturally compact grower, the plant usually stays under 2 feet (60cm), and some of the cultivars are even smaller. (One, 'Christmas Tree', is a mere 8 inches [20.5cm] tall.) The plant readily lends itself to formal edging schemes and is also a superb choice for carpeting the area under tall trees.

Its only drawback is its vulnerability to snails and slugs. So if these pests are in residence in your garden, be prepared to protect your lilyturf.

As the name suggests, the blooms look like taller versions of the spring-flowering bulb *Muscari*, also known as grape hyacinth. They appear on narrow 10- to 20-inch (25.5 to 51cm) spikes late in the season, and are generally purple, though white varieties also exist.

Lobelia cardinalis

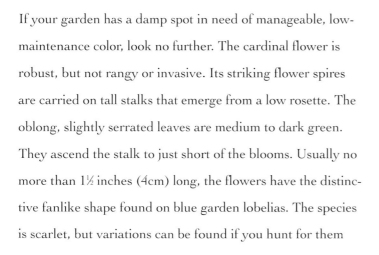

Cardinal flower

BLOOM TIME: mid–late summer

HEIGHT/WIDTH: 3′–5′ × 1′ (90cm–1.5m × 30cm)

LIGHT: full sun–full shade

ZONES: 2–9

Cardinal flower

If your garden has a damp spot in need of manageable, low-maintenance color, look no further. The cardinal flower is robust, but not rangy or invasive. Its striking flower spires are carried on tall stalks that emerge from a low rosette. The oblong, slightly serrated leaves are medium to dark green. They ascend the stalk to just short of the blooms. Usually no more than 1½ inches (4cm) long, the flowers have the distinctive fanlike shape found on blue garden lobelias. The species is scarlet, but variations can be found if you hunt for them (some may be crosses with other, similar lobelias). 'Ruby Slippers' is an especially gorgeous choice, as is the richly hued, more subtle 'Garnet'. There's also a white ('Alba') and a soft pink ('Heather Pink'), and many others.

Although this handsome native North American plant is found growing along streams and ponds in the wild, such naturally wet conditions are not mandatory. It will adapt well to the garden proper, just so long as the soil is moist or you water often and mulch.

Lupinus

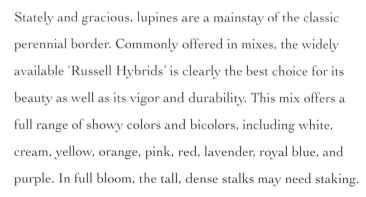

Lupine

BLOOM TIME: late spring–early summer

HEIGHT/WIDTH: 3'–4' × 1½'–2' (90–120cm × 45–60cm)

LIGHT: full sun–partial shade

ZONES: 4–8

Lupine

Stately and gracious, lupines are a mainstay of the classic perennial border. Commonly offered in mixes, the widely available 'Russell Hybrids' is clearly the best choice for its beauty as well as its vigor and durability. This mix offers a full range of showy colors and bicolors, including white, cream, yellow, orange, pink, red, lavender, royal blue, and purple. In full bloom, the tall, dense stalks may need staking.

Even the foliage of lupines is beautiful. It's lance-shaped, between 6 and 12 inches (15 and 30cm) long, and gathered in palmate leaflets. The leaves have a light coating of tiny silky hairs that capture water droplets—a truly fetching sight.

The secret to growing spectacular lupines is in the soil; it should be deep, moist yet well drained, acidic, and moderately rich. These plants are very sensitive to hot, dry weather—a mulch and some shade may help, but they won't be able to take too much of that sort of stress.

Lychnis coronaria

Rose campion

BLOOM TIME: early summer

HEIGHT/WIDTH: 2′–3′ × 1½′ (60–90cm × 45cm)

LIGHT: full sun

ZONES: 4–8

Rose campion

There's nothing else quite like these flowers: they're a bold, vivid shade of pink, almost fluorescent. The easygoing plant produces them in great numbers, so although each flower is only 1 inch (2.5cm) across, the effect is bright and vivacious. Fuzzy, grayish white foliage makes a cool, calming contrast to the loud flowers and lends interest to a border when the plant is not blooming. The plant has rather a loose profile and is multibranched. It may sprawl. Rose campion is rarely long-lived, but it self-sows, so you'll never lose it.

Needless to say, such an unusual-looking plant is not easy to combine with others. You might tuck it into a spot where later-blooming plants won't overlap with it. Or try it in an herb garden setting, or among other gray-leaved plants.

Lysimachia clethroides

Gooseneck loosestrife

BLOOM TIME: summer

HEIGHT/WIDTH: 2'–3' × 3' (60–90cm × 90cm)

LIGHT: full sun–partial shade

ZONES: 3–9

Gooseneck loosestrife

To say that gooseneck loosestrife is easy to grow would be an understatement. Some gardeners find it downright invasive, especially in moist soils. But it is a great beauty. So if you have a spot where this tendency will not be a problem (say, an area under the high shade of trees in need of brightening), go ahead and plant it.

The common name refers to the slender white spikes, which arch over at their tips. This quality becomes absolutely charming when the plant is grown in groups. One writer has likened the sight to "a flock of eager geese on the run." The spikes vary from a mere 3 inches (7.5cm) long to a generous 12 inches (30.5cm). Close inspection reveals that they are composed of dozens of tiny, densely packed flowers. As for the leaves, they're a basic, tapered oval shape, slightly furry, and line the stems right up the base of the flower spikes. The plant's profile is lush and casual.

Malva alcea

Hollyhock mallow

BLOOM TIME: midsummer–autumn

HEIGHT/WIDTH: 3′–4′ × 1′–2′ (90–120cm × 30–60cm)

LIGHT: full sun

ZONES: 4–9

'Fastigiata' hollyhock mallow

Malva alcea is not really a hollyhock at all. But this bushy, long-blooming plant deserves to be as widely grown as the hollyhock. It is perfect for the middle of a sunny border or even a container on a porch or deck. Easygoing and drought-tolerant, it is also incredibly generous with its saucer-shaped blooms. They're about 2 inches (5cm) across, and usually a sweet rose pink with darker veining and a cream-colored center. They literally envelop the entire plant for weeks on end. The sometimes lax stems are lined with rather dainty, lobed palmate leaves. The plant owes its tough constitution to a thick, fibrous root system. And if that doesn't assure its survival in your garden, its propensity to self-sow will.

The most widely available form is a cultivar named 'Fastigiata', which is a neater, more upright plant. But, like the species, it may need to be staked later in the season.

Mertensia virginica

Virginia bluebells

BLOOM TIME: spring

HEIGHT/WIDTH: 1′–2′ × 1½′ (30–60cm × 45cm)

LIGHT: partial–full shade

ZONES: 3–9

Virginia bluebells

Looking for a sweet companion for your spring-flowering bulbs? Something versatile and dependable? Virginia bluebells may be your perennial. A native of southeastern woodlands, it likes similar conditions in the garden: organically rich soil in cool shade. The thin, lance-shaped leaves are mainly basal, but also ascend the stems on short, succulent stalks. At the top of these stalks are clusters of nodding little bells. They begin as pink buds, then open to lilac-blue flowers. The blue will be darker in deeper shade. In any case, the color seems to go with everything, but is particularly fetching combined with small-flowered yellow or white narcissus.

Like the bulbs, though, Virginia bluebells' show ends as summer arrives. The stems die down after bloom, and the plant gradually goes dormant and disappears from view, until next year. So mark its spot if you wish to move or divide it in the autumn, and to avoid trampling it or planting something else right above it.

Monarda didyma

Bee balm

BLOOM TIME: mid–late summer

HEIGHT/WIDTH: 2½'–3' × 1½' (75–90cm × 45cm)

LIGHT: full sun–partial shade

ZONES: 4–9

'Cambridge Scarlet' bee balm

This showy relative of mint is just as easy to grow, so long as your garden has the rich, moist soil it needs to thrive. Like mint, it has aromatic dark green leaves and square stems, and can be invasive (keep it in bounds by chopping back at the roots' outer perimeter). The big flower heads, up to 4 inches (10cm) across, are a knockout in full bloom. And hummingbirds find them irresistible.

It is most often seen in scarlet ('Cambridge Scarlet', 'Gardenview Scarlet'), but recent years have seen a flurry of new introductions in other colors. 'Marshall's Delight' is peppermint pink, 'Raspberry Wine' is a clear, unmuddied wine red, 'Claire Grace' is lavender, and 'Snow Queen' is pure white. All offer wonderful possibilities for perennial border combinations, and also look terrific in each other's company.

Traditionally, this stalwart plant has been susceptible to mildew, which disfigures it later in the season. Breeders are well aware of this problem, however, and many of the new varieties mentioned above, while not immune, are touted as "resistant." You can do your part by offering each plant enough elbow room to allow for air circulation, and spraying with a sulfur fungicide if need be.

Nepeta × faassenii

Catmint

BLOOM TIME: early–midsummer

HEIGHT/WIDTH: 1'–1½' × 1½' (30–45cm × 45cm)

LIGHT: full sun

ZONES: 4–9

Catmint

Some herblike plants for the garden are a little rangy or sparse flowering. But this is not true of the robust, free-blooming catmint. It produces many generous spires of small, light purple, long-lasting flowers that always look perky and fresh. The fragrant foliage below is a neat gray-green.

The best thing about this plant, though, is its habit. Despite its profuse blooms, it has a natural grace and remains compact and tidy looking. You could certainly use it as an edging in the front of a border, along a path, or in front of rosebushes or other shrubs. Or try massing it as an unusual groundcover in a sunny spot. After the catmint is finished flowering, some gardeners chop it back about halfway. This keeps it neat and may inspire a second round of blooms later in the summer.

Oenothera tetragona

Yellow evening primrose, sundrops

BLOOM TIME: early summer

HEIGHT/WIDTH: 2' × 1' (60cm × 30cm)

LIGHT: full sun

ZONES: 4–8

Yellow evening primrose

Few other plants offer the exuberant bright yellow that you get from this clump-forming, but sprawling, plant. Evening primrose sends up fuzzy branched stems that bear spikes of butter yellow, cup-shaped 1- to 2-inch (2.5 to 5cm) blooms in early summer. 'Fireworks' is an improved variety with slightly bigger flowers; it also flowers longer and often has an autumn encore. Other closely related species that are worth growing include *O. fruticosa* and *O. missouriensis* and cultivars of them. Some of these have reddish stems or buds,

which add to the plant's overall appeal. You may well be tempted to combine evening primroses with blue or purple flowers, but try it also with yellow-centered white daisies for a fresh-looking display.

Evening primrose is not particular about soil, and will do well in moist or dry settings. However, don't let it sit in saturated, poorly drained soil or it will succumb to rot. It is drought-tolerant and untroubled by pests and diseases.

Paeonia

Herbaceous peony

BLOOM TIME: spring

HEIGHT/WIDTH: 1½'–3½' × 2'–3' (45–105cm × 60–90cm)

LIGHT: full sun

ZONES: 3–7

'Largo' herbaceous peony

If you live where the winters are long and cold (Zones 3 and 4), you already know your choices of hardy perennials are somewhat limited, and you would be crazy not to grow peonies. Even if you live further south, you would be crazy not to grow them. Peonies have a well-deserved reputation for being as tough as they are gorgeous. The double-flowered varieties are more popular, but the single-flowered ones offer a contrasting center boss of golden stamens. Some new hybrids sport a tuft of extra petals at the center of the bloom. All peonies have handsome divided foliage that is an asset to the garden long after the blooms are gone.

Generally derived from *P. lactiflora* and *P. officinalis*, the hybrids are legion. One of the oldest and still one of the best is the sweetly fragrant 'Festiva Maxima', which has plush white blooms flecked with crimson. Another favorite is the deliciously scented, soft pink 'Sarah Bernhardt'. Do yourself a favor and order a fall catalog (because peonies should be planted in autumn) from a peony specialist or a perennial nursery that devotes many pages to this group.

There's no real mystery to growing fabulous peonies. Just plant the stout rootstocks 1 or 2 inches (2.5 to 5cm) deep in organically rich, well-drained soil.

Papaver orientale

Oriental poppy

BLOOM TIME: early summer

HEIGHT/WIDTH: 2'–4' × 2'–3' (60–120cm × 60–90cm)

LIGHT: full sun

ZONES: 3–7

Oriental poppy

They may look exotic, but Oriental poppies are no trouble to grow. Just plant them in light or heavy well-drained soil. The large, 4- to 6-inch (10 to 15cm) crepe-paper blossoms open to a graceful goblet shape. When the blossoms are open, you will see black accent markings at the petal bases and a fat, distinctive center mound of stamens. The effect is sensational, especially in the fiery red- and orange-flowered varieties. But the drama is not lost on the pink-flowered varieties either. If you cut some for bouquets, you'll notice a milky sap. Stop the flow and assure longer vase life by searing the cut base with a lit match.

The light green, furry foliage is rather rough looking, but the flowers steal the show anyway. By midsummer, the plant dies back and fades away. The best way to capitalize on Oriental poppy's brief but exciting show is to use it to bridge the gap between spring-flowering bulbs and summer bloomers. A popular and successful perennial companion is baby's-breath (*Gypsophila*), which begins to bloom just as the Oriental poppies fade and quickly billows over the gaps they leave behind.

Penstemon digitalis

Foxglove penstemon

BLOOM TIME: early summer

HEIGHT/WIDTH: 2′–5′ × 2′–3′ (60cm–1.5m × 60–90cm)

LIGHT: full sun

ZONES: 4–8

'Husker Red' foxglove penstemon

There are many species of penstemon, and they all share a more or less erect profile and arching, unbranched spires of small, pretty tubular flowers. But some are tricky to grow well outside of their native habitat (usually the mountains of the West). Foxglove penstemon is one of the more adaptable species. Taller than some of its relatives, it starts from a tufted rosette on the ground, then sends up stout stalks lined with long, lance-shaped leaves. These are topped with jaunty clusters of 1-inch (2.5cm) flowers.

The cultivar 'Husker Red' recently won the Perennial Plant Association's "Plant of the Year" award, an honor bestowed on a perennial that is considered superior and particularly easy to grow. The name 'Husker Red' comes from the reddish foliage and stems. The flowers are white, but sometimes they develop a pink cast. Like all penstemons, *P. digitalis* cannot tolerate sodden soil, so plant it in a well-drained spot. The fibrous root system will help it through periods of drought.

Perovskia atriplicifolia

Russian sage

BLOOM TIME: midsummer–autumn

HEIGHT/WIDTH: $3' \times 2'$ (90×60cm)

LIGHT: full sun

ZONES: 5–7

Russian sage

Always fresh-looking, always pretty, Russian sage is a great addition to any perennial garden. Great spires of fuzzy, soft lilac-blue flowers bloom for weeks on end in late summer. And silvery gray, cut-leaf foliage emits a pleasant, sagelike scent when handled. This enchanting combination seems to enhance many other colors, from darker purple blooms to softest pink to pastel yellow. The branches also make a splendid contribution to homegrown bouquets.

Because it is broad and bushy, and develops woody stems over time, Russian sage might be taken for a shrub. But in order to encourage the best performance, you should cut it back to the ground in late autumn or early spring so new growth can take the stage. Truly a trouble-free plant, it is immune to pests and withstands heat and drought with style.

Phlox paniculata

Summer phlox

BLOOM TIME: midsummer

HEIGHT/WIDTH: 2′–5′ × 2′ (60cm–1.5m × 60cm)

LIGHT: full sun

ZONES: 3–9

Summer phlox

For a carnival of bright, lively color and a bonus of sweet scent, summer phlox is hard to beat. The hybrids come in a broad range of hues, from snowy white to pink, red, lavender, and purple. Many have a contrasting center eye that adds extra sparkle. If you have the space, by all means plant a mixture. Otherwise, you are sure to find at least one or two individual varieties that capture your imagination and fit well into your garden's color scheme. One of the best is 'Bright Eyes', pastel pink with a crimson center— plant it near purple liatris or blue echinops. If you prefer a solid-color phlox, try beet red 'Starfire' or all-white 'David'.

Phlox bloom heavily for weeks on end, provided they're planted in rich soil and get plenty of water. Their only flaw is susceptibility to powdery mildew, which attacks the plants toward the end of the season. A little extra room for air circulation may help. Plant individuals fairly well apart at the outset or do some thinning after the plants are up and growing in the spring. Spraying with an "anti-transpirant" (a product used to prevent foliage from dehydrating—ask at your local garden center) also seems to help. An easier recourse, though, is to plant resistant varieties. Ask for them, or read catalog descriptions carefully.

Platycodon grandiflorus

Balloon flower

BLOOM TIME: summer

HEIGHT/WIDTH: 1½'–2½' × 1' (45–75cm × 30cm)

LIGHT: full sun–partial shade

ZONES: 3–9

Balloon flower

This easygoing, attractive plant gets its name from its buds, which puff out like balloons prior to popping open. The flowers are cup-shaped, and are about 2 inches (5cm) across. They look a lot like campanulas, which is no surprise, since they're in the same family. At any given point over the course of the summer, you'll have both buds and open blooms on the same plant, making for a fun and pretty display. If you deadhead regularly, the blooms will keep on coming. Another plus: the plants will self-sow. Balloon flower provides lots of reliable color in perennial borders.

And you'll find that the blue mixes well with many other colors. You might wish to try other cultivars—balloon flower also comes in pink and white.

Balloon flower demands little of the gardener. It will grow in a variety of soils, but is at its best in sandy, well-drained soil. Note that it is slow to come up in the spring—don't give up on it (it is very hardy). The thick roots help the plant endure periods of drought but also make transplanting tricky.

Polygonatum commutatum

Great Solomon's-seal

BLOOM TIME: spring

HEIGHT/WIDTH: 3'–5' × 2'–3' (90cm–1.5m ×
60–90cm)

LIGHT: partial–full shade

ZONES: 4–8

Great Solomon's-seal

One of the finest and easiest of all shade plants, Solomon's-seal has a wonderful presence in the garden. Strong, gracefully arching stems spread outward, bearing along their length oval-shaped, parallel-veined leaves. In the spring, a jaunty row of lightly perfumed, pale green to white, bell-shaped flowers dangle along the undersides of the stems. These become blue-black berries by late summer.

This is the largest of the Solomon's-seals. If your garden is smaller, you'll find very similar ones that are up to half the size. Or try the closely related, medium-size *P. odoratum* cultivar 'Variegatum', whose leaf edges and tips are splashed with white markings.

In any case, this plant is eager to please. Just give it the woodland soil and shade it prefers, and enjoy the show. If you are building a many-textured shade display, note that great Solomon's-seal combines well with hostas and ferns.

Potentilla atrosanguinea

Himalayan cinquefoil

BLOOM TIME: early summer

HEIGHT/WIDTH: 1½'–2' × 1'–2' (45–60cm × 30–60cm)

LIGHT: full sun

ZONES: 5–8

Himalayan cinquefoil

This groundcovering potentilla is a relative of the bigger, mounding shrubs. It offers a season of attractive foliage and, in late spring, especially vivid color. It grows densely, outcompeting weeds, and spreads gradually, so it's easy to keep in bounds. The medium green foliage, underlaid with silver, consists of compact rosettes of five-fingered leaflets. The 1-inch (2.5cm) red flowers come in clusters. Among the cultivars are some real knockouts, many of which are longer-blooming than the species. Try 'Gibson's Scarlet' (bright red), 'William Rollison' (semidouble, fiery orange and yellow), or 'Fire Dance' (salmon red, edged in yellow).

Use Himalayan cinquefoil in rock garden settings, or plant a row along the front of a warm-colored perennial border. It grows best in fertile soil, is untroubled by pests and diseases, and is happy in sun or part shade. There's only one catch: it struggles in areas with very hot summers or very cold winters.

Primula japonica

Japanese primrose, candelabra primrose

BLOOM TIME: spring

HEIGHT/WIDTH: 1'–2' × 1' (30–60cm × 30cm)

LIGHT: partial shade

ZONES: 5–8

Japanese primrose

Of all the beautiful members of the large primrose family, the Japanese primrose is perhaps the easiest to grow. It does require a cool climate, shade, and damp soil, but once these basic needs are met, it will flourish. In fact, it is likely to self-sow, so you might as well plan to devote a broad area to this enthusiastic plant.

The flowers are unique. They line the stalks on all sides, in whorls, and appear in tiers, not just at the top. Individual blossoms are a mere ½ inch (1.5cm) across, but they are clustered so there's no missing them. The flowers range from white to pink to lavender, and are accented with contrasting eyes (darker pink or red, sometimes yellow). As with other primroses, the leaves remain basal (that is, at ground level) and are broadly paddle-shaped.

Combine Japanese primroses with other shade-lovers, but try to stay with foliage plants such as ferns or hostas. You won't want anything to distract from these sensational flowers.

Pulmonaria saccharata

Bethlehem sage

BLOOM TIME: spring

HEIGHT/WIDTH: 9"–1½' × 2' (23–45cm × 60cm)

LIGHT: partial–full shade

ZONES: 3–8

'Mrs. Moon' Bethlehem sage

Large, sturdy leaves dappled with silvery spots and blotches make this groundcovering plant stand out in the shade. The leaves are mostly basal and lance-shaped, and can grow up to 1 foot (30cm) long and 6 inches (15cm) wide. In mild climates, the leaves may weather the winter. When planted en masse, Bethlehem sage forms an elegant, luminous carpet. Do give it shade—the more, the better—and moisture is essential as well. One of its favorite spots is under the shade of tall deciduous trees.

The blossoms, while fleeting, are lovely. Loose clusters of rosy pink buds open to sweet, violet-blue bells. The most widely available variety, 'Mrs. Moon', has pink flowers that age to blue and more prominently spotted leaves. 'Sissinghurst White' has white flowers.

Bethlehem sage is easy to incorporate into a spring bulb display, and the leaves will remain to help disguise the fading bulb foliage. It's also nice with other spring-blooming perennials, particularly white-flowered bleeding-heart.

Rudbeckia fulgida

Black-eyed Susan

BLOOM TIME: midsummer–autumn

HEIGHT/WIDTH: 2′ × 2′ (60cm × 60cm)

LIGHT: full sun

ZONES: 3–10

'Goldsturm' black-eyed Susan

Perennials don't get any easier than this tough, bright, long-blooming daisy. The plant smothers itself in 2- to 3-inch (5 to 7.5cm) blooms for weeks on end. Vibrant, yellow-orange petals surround a chocolate brown center. These not only keep well on the plant but make for exceptional summertime bouquets. The rough-textured leaves are an attractive oval to lance shape. They are a neat, contrasting shade of dark green. The plants don't get leggy, don't flop, and don't give up in heat and drought conditions. A superior selection with even larger flowers (to 4 inches [10cm] across) and a more compact habit is *R. fulgida* var. *sullivantii* 'Goldsturm'.

There are many ways to use this terrific plant. The popular "new American garden" look (not so new now, but still in vogue) pairs it with plain and variegated ornamental grasses for a display that is both exciting and casual. But it is just as easily combined with flowering partners, preferably also in bold colors, such as red bee balm.

Ruta graveolens

Rue

BLOOM TIME: summer

HEIGHT/WIDTH: 1′–3′ × 1′–2′ (30–90cm × 30–60cm)

LIGHT: full sun

ZONES: 4–9

Rue

A mound-forming foliage plant, rue has beautiful, smooth blue-green leaves. Individual leaves are rather small and almost spoon-shaped. They are borne in symmetrical leaflets that are much divided, giving the plant an almost fernlike delicacy. You can promote a bushier, more compact habit by pruning back the plant each spring.

The soft-hued leaves provide a wonderful cooling effect in sunny borders where silver-leaved foliage plants aren't appropriate. Try interplanting with blue-flowered campanu-las or verbenas for a stunning show. (The small, not especially striking mustard yellow flowers appear in early summer to midsummer. If they don't appeal to you, they can be easily removed.)

Rue is gratifyingly easy to grow. It likes sandy or loamy soil best, and is drought-tolerant. Pests and diseases never bother it. The only thing to watch out for is contracting dermatitis when handling the plants—some people develop a rash.

Salvia

Sage

BLOOM TIME: summer

HEIGHT/WIDTH: varies

LIGHT: full sun

ZONES: 4–9

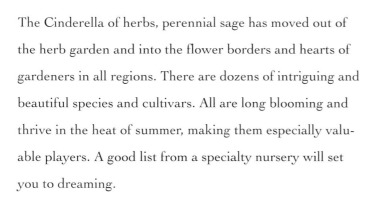

'May Night' sage

The Cinderella of herbs, perennial sage has moved out of the herb garden and into the flower borders and hearts of gardeners in all regions. There are dozens of intriguing and beautiful species and cultivars. All are long blooming and thrive in the heat of summer, making them especially valuable players. A good list from a specialty nursery will set you to dreaming.

Among the many worthy choices are some especially dramatic flowering selections. *Salvia coccinea* adorns its 1- to 2-foot (30 to 60cm) stalks with remarkable scarlet blooms accented with purple. The slightly taller *S. × superba* (1½ to 3 feet [45 to 90cm]) features stunning hybrids with dense flower spikes—look for royal purple 'East Friesland' or maroon-tinged purple 'May Night'. Autumn-blooming *Salvia leucantha* 'Emerald' grows to 4 feet (1.2m) tall and has red-violet buds that open to reveal white petals.

Generally speaking, these salvias are clump-forming plants with woody bases. They have gray-green to green foliage (which may be scented), and their flower spires appear in profusion above the leaves. Some spires are sturdy and erect, suggesting use in a formal setting, while others are arching wands perfect for casual plantings.

Scabiosa columbaria

Pincushion flower

BLOOM TIME: summer

HEIGHT/WIDTH: 1½′–2′ × 1½′–2′ (45–60cm × 45–60cm)

LIGHT: full sun

ZONES: 5–10

'Butterfly Blue' pincushion flower

This little charmer is a hard worker. It produces clouds of lacy 1½-inch (4cm) blooms for most of the summer, especially if you deadhead or pick for bouquets. The plants maintain themselves as tidy clumps and have slightly fuzzy stems and small, cut leaflets of sage green. 'Butterfly Blue' is widely sold and is actually more lavender than blue; 'Pink Mist' is also available. Use both together to bring an instant, cottage garden feel to your yard. Pincushion flowers are also perfect for tucking into a perennial border where all-season color is desired.

Encourage pincushion flower's exuberant performance by planting it in full sun in a light, loamy soil that is toward the alkaline side. It doesn't like excessive heat and humidity, but southern gardeners may have success if there's some cooling afternoon shade.

Sedum spectabile

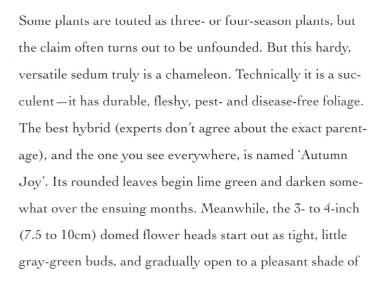

Stonecrop

BLOOM TIME: late summer

HEIGHT/WIDTH: 1½'–2' × 1½' (45–60cm × 45cm)

LIGHT: full sun–partial shade

ZONES: 4–9

'Autumn Joy' stonecrop

Some plants are touted as three- or four-season plants, but the claim often turns out to be unfounded. But this hardy, versatile sedum truly is a chameleon. Technically it is a succulent—it has durable, fleshy, pest- and disease-free foliage. The best hybrid (experts don't agree about the exact parentage), and the one you see everywhere, is named 'Autumn Joy'. Its rounded leaves begin lime green and darken somewhat over the ensuing months. Meanwhile, the 3- to 4-inch (7.5 to 10cm) domed flower heads start out as tight, little gray-green buds, and gradually open to a pleasant shade of pink. As autumn approaches, the flowers start to turn rosy red, then russet, and finally, rust brown. If your winters are not overly harsh, the rust brown heads will remain all through the cold weather. Other cultivars with flower heads in variations of pink and red are also available.

Plant this sedum in decent, well-drained soil. Don't overwater. In fact, don't fuss much over this low-maintenance classic. With very little effort or intervention on your part, it will delight for years to come.

Solidago

Ornamental goldenrod

BLOOM TIME: midsummer–autumn

HEIGHT/WIDTH: varies

LIGHT: full sun

ZONES: 3–9

Ornamental goldenrod

If you think this is a weed plant, look again. Nowadays, thanks more to European horticulturists than to North American ones, there are some terrific hybrids. The best are well behaved enough to stay in bounds in your perennial borders, and feature glorious plumes composed of tiny golden flowers. The only thing they share with their wild cousins is an eagerness to bloom and easy maintenance. There's nothing quite like them in late summer. In both color and form, they make a great contribution to the garden. You'll love them with the yellow-centered Michaelmas daisies (New England asters).

Nurseries that specialize in native plants carry many of these desirable goldenrods. The aptly named *S. rugosa* 'Fireworks' is a compact, dome-shaped, clump-forming plant (3 to 4 feet [90 to 120cm] tall) that cascades with bright yellow color. *S. sphacelata* 'Golden Fleece' is a dwarf selection (1½ to 2 feet [45 to 60cm] tall) that carries its cheery sprays in a tidy, pyramidal fashion. *S. virgaurea* 'Crown of Rays' (2 feet [60cm] tall) has such full, lush plumes that it looks like a golden waterfall. All of these do well in poor-to-average soil—in fact, soil that is too rich will cause them to grow more rampantly than you might wish.

Stachys byzantina

Lamb's-ears

BLOOM TIME: late spring

HEIGHT/WIDTH: 1'–1½' × 1' (45cm × 30cm)

LIGHT: full sun–partial shade

ZONES: 4–9

Lamb's-ears

This silver-leaved plant is a perennial garden classic, and with good reason. So long as it is growing in poor-to-average soil, it will produce wonderful oblong leaves in a consistently lovely shade of silvery gray. The sweet name comes from the texture, which is as soft as felt ... or a lamb's ear.

Because the plant likes to sprawl, it is perfect for soft edging along a path or planter. Or include it in a casual flower border, with pink, lavender, purple, or red perennials or roses. It is also lovely interwoven with irises—it seems to go with all types and colors.

Although some gardeners don't like lamb-ear's blooms and cut them off as soon as they appear, the flowers are hardly offensive. Stout, woolly spikes bear lavender flowers that pass by the time summer is in full swing. If you're in the antiflower camp, you can always grow a nonflowering cultivar. 'Silver Carpet' is considered the best one.

Stokesia laevis

Stokes' aster

BLOOM TIME: summer

HEIGHT/WIDTH: 1′–2′ × 1′–2′ (30–60cm × 30–60cm)

LIGHT: full sun

ZONES: 5–9

Stokes' aster

Although the blooms of Stokes' aster are wonderfully intricate and delicate looking, they are durable and long lasting, and borne on a tough, vigorous plant. The flower heads are about 4 inches (10cm) across, and feature two rows of numerous petals. The outer petals spray outward in a loose, open fashion, while the shorter, inner ones hug close to the center. The effect is reminiscent of a Chinese aster or a bachelor's button. In any event, they're produced one to a stalk, which is convenient for bouquet-lovers. They also tend to have a long vase life. The species is usually lavender-blue, but there are many fine cultivars. 'Alba', of course, has white flowers. 'Klaus Jelitto' has powder blue blooms. Those of 'Wyoming' are dark blue.

The plant itself is a mound-former, and covered in smooth, spear-shaped leaves that make a nice contrast to the interesting flowers. It is no trouble to grow, and is happiest in soil that is neither too fertile nor too poor. Just avoid letting its area get waterlogged during the winter and don't overwater it.

Thalictrum aquilegifolium

Meadow rue

BLOOM TIME: late spring

HEIGHT/WIDTH: 2′–3′ × 1′ (60–90cm × 30cm)

LIGHT: full sun–partial shade

ZONES: 5–9

Meadow rue

Meadow rue greets spring with powder-puff lavender blooms atop slender, swaying stalks. If lavender doesn't fit in your color plans, look for the white version, 'Alba'. *T. aquilegifolium* is shorter than the other species and doesn't require staking. But it is still tall enough to bring a little height to the middle or back of a flower bed. The "aquilegifolium" part of the name refers to the fact that the dainty, lacy leaves are similar to those of *Aquilegia* (columbine).

These are bluish green and clothe the stems at loose intervals, stopping short of the flower heads. Thanks to the leaves, the plant remains a welcome, graceful presence in the garden even after the flowers have come and gone.

The key to a sterling performance from meadow rue is moist soil, which is what it has in its native habitat. A light mulch and some afternoon shade is a good idea, especially in areas with hot summers.

Tradescantia × andersoniana

Spiderwort

BLOOM TIME: summer

HEIGHT/WIDTH: 1½'–3' × 2' (45–90cm × 60cm)

LIGHT: full sun

ZONES: 5–9

Spiderwort

Spiderwort's clumps of grassy, spear-shaped foliage will enthusiastically cover a sunny bank or serve as a foundation planting. And it has the added bonus of a constant supply of flowers. The leaves can be as long as 1 foot (30cm). They interweave and overlap, generally to the exclusion of weeds. The distinctive, three-petaled flowers look a bit like little tricorner colonial hats. Centered with a small boss of yellow-tipped stamens, they are carried in umbels. About 1½ inches (4cm) across, the flowers are usually a vivid shade of purple, but almost-blue hybrids exist, as do crisp white and rich magenta ones. All appear over a very long period, for weeks or even months. Deadheading is not necessary—the petals fade and drop unobtrusively. If the show begins to dissipate, simply cut back the entire plant hard; by autumn, you should get a repeat performance.

A truly low-maintenance plant, spiderwort is perfectly content with soil that is so poor nothing else seems to thrive in it. Feeding and regular watering are not a good idea, unless you want to encourage excessive foliage growth.

Trollius × cultorum

Globeflower

BLOOM TIME: late spring

HEIGHT/WIDTH: 2′–3′ × 1′ (60–90cm × 30cm)

LIGHT: full sun–partial shade

ZONES: 3–9

Globeflower

Extra-hardy and extra-vibrant, globeflowers are a wonderful choice for locations with moist soil. Once that basic soil need is met, they are sure to bloom for weeks. Regular deadheading will extend the performance even further. The traditionally yellow blossoms begin as fat, round buds. They spring open to become many-petaled, 1- to 2-inch (2.5 to 5cm), globe-shaped blooms that look a bit like tiny lotus blossoms (though trollius is actually cousin to the buttercup). Because the flowers are usually borne on single, strong stalks, they are a natural for sweet, cheerful bouquets.

The plant forms rather loose, open clumps. The attractive foliage is dark green, palmate, deeply divided, and lines the stems at intervals. A slow grower, globeflower will stay easily within the bounds you allot it.

Some exciting cultivars have appeared in recent years and are as easy to grow as the species. The bicolor 'Be Mine' has butter yellow outer petals and a rich orange center. 'Alabaster' has creamy white blooms. And 'Fireglobe' has fiery orange-yellow flowers.

Verbascum chaixii

Nettle-leaved mullein

BLOOM TIME: summer

HEIGHT/WIDTH: 2'–3' × 1½' (60–90cm × 45cm)

LIGHT: full sun

ZONES: 6–9

'Album' nettle-leaved mullein

This is a terrific plant for the middle of a border, especially in the company of purple or blue flowers. Unlike some of its weedy roadside relatives, *V. chaixii* has nice foliage and numerous densely blooming flower stalks. It does retain a preference for well-drained or even dry soil and is easy to grow. This species is perennial, while many other mulleins are short-lived biennials.

The yellow flowers centered with woolly purple-to-maroon stamens are up to 1 inch (2.5cm) across. A wonderful cultivar named 'Album' has white petals and the same attractive centers. It is ideal for a cottage garden setting with other soft-colored flowers.

The sage green leaves, which are 3 to 6 inches (7.5 to 15cm) long, and the strong stems are both coated with a soft fuzz. The best thing about this plant is its stately profile. It always holds itself erect, and never needs staking. However, if you plant it in anything less than full sun, the stalks will bend and contort themselves in their efforts to reach for the sun.

Veronica spicata

Spike speedwell

BLOOM TIME: summer

HEIGHT/WIDTH: 1'–2' × 1'–2' (30–60cm × 30–60cm)

LIGHT: full sun–partial shade

ZONES: 4–9

'Red Fox' spike speedwell

Veronica is an upright-growing plant that doesn't get very tall. It is ideal for edging a walk, and well suited to life in a sunny perennial border. Sporting handsome spires of blue-purple blooms, it looks terrific for up to two months running in early summer to midsummer. And diligent dead-heading will prolong the show. The plant spreads out a bit, but has a neat appearance. The lance-shaped, tapered leaves are only about 2 inches (5cm) long and are usually a nice, contrasting matte green.

Veronica is simple to grow. It prefers moderation in all things—moderate soil, not too damp or too dry, and does just as well in full sun as in partial shade. No pests or diseases ever trouble it.

This agreeable plant also comes in colors other than blue-purple. The especially long-blooming 'Icicle' is pure white, and 'Red Fox' is a splendid shade of rosy red. If you have an exact color scheme in mind, you will be happy to learn that there are gradations of shade between blue and purple. The best of these is dark blue 'Sunny Border Blue', which was the Perennial Plant Association's "Plant of the Year" in 1993.

Viola odorata

Sweet violet

BLOOM TIME: spring

HEIGHT/WIDTH: 2″–8″ × 8″ (5.0–20.5cm × 20.5cm)

LIGHT: partial shade

ZONES: 6–9

Sweet violet

This dainty, fragrant violet immediately conjures up visions of Victorian-style Valentine's Day cards. The little leaves, 2 to 3 inches (5 to 7.5cm) long, are appropriately heart-shaped. Unlike some other violets, the flowers rise directly from the center of the plant on short stems. They're only about ¾ inches (2cm) across, but appear in great numbers and waft such an enticing perfume into the air that you almost forget how small they are. Traditionally violet, you can also find *Viola odorata* in other enchanting colors: 'White Czar' is pure white, 'Rosina' is rose pink, and 'Royal Robe' is a deep dark blue.

The most appropriate use of sweet violets is in a woodland setting, where they can enjoy the cool, moist soil and semishade they need to thrive. When happy, they will spread eagerly, making for a sweet groundcover. You can also employ them as edging for a shady border. But your greatest joy in growing these will be slipping out to pick a handful for a bouquet for the house or as a gift.

PLANT HARDINESS ZONES

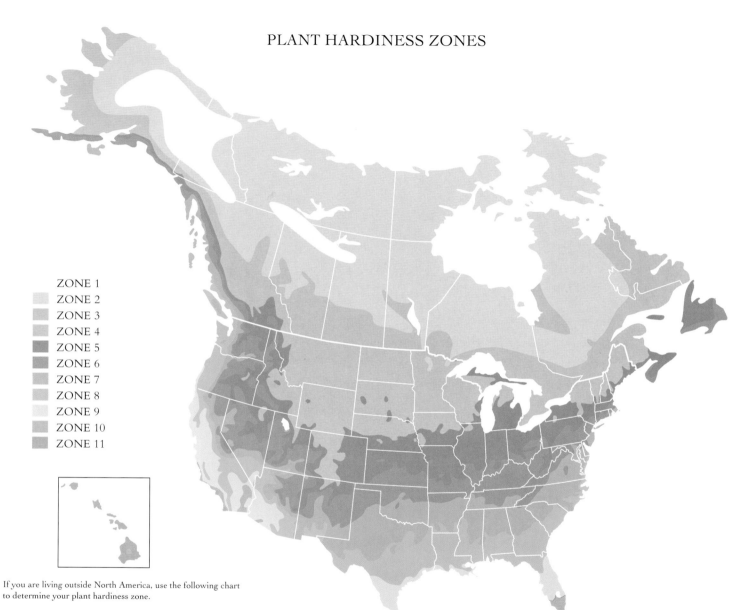

ZONE 1
ZONE 2
ZONE 3
ZONE 4
ZONE 5
ZONE 6
ZONE 7
ZONE 8
ZONE 9
ZONE 10
ZONE 11

If you are living outside North America, use the following chart to determine your plant hardiness zone.

Range of Average Annual Minimum Temperatures for Each Zone

	Fahrenheit (°F)	Celsius (°C)
Zone 1	Below −50°	Below −45.6°
Zone 2	−50° to −40°	−45.6° to −40°
Zone 3	−40° to −30°	−40° to −34.4°
Zone 4	−30° to −20°	−34.4° to −28.9°
Zone 5	−20° to −10°	−28.9° to −23.3°
Zone 6	−10° to 0°	−23.3° to −17.8°
Zone 7	0° to 10°	−17.8° to −12.2°
Zone 8	10° to 20°	−12.2° to −6.7°
Zone 9	20° to 30°	−6.7° to −1.1°
Zone 10	30° to 40°	−1.1° to 4.4°
Zone 11	Above 40°	Above 4.4°

Sources

Shop for your garden by mail, and you will find a much broader selection than you ever dreamed of! Don't forget to send the appropriate catalog fee with your request, as some of the nurseries listed below are small operations, and need to cover their printing costs. Also, be sure to write your request neatly so they can make out your address.

For further help and ideas, look for this splendid book at your local bookstore, or special-order it:

Gardening By Mail: A Source Book
4th edition, updated and revised
Barbara J. Barton
Houghton-Mifflin, 1994
$21.00 paperback

Mail-order sources for perennial plants:

Bluestone Perennials
7237 Middle Ridge Road
Madison, OH 44057
Free catalog

Busse Gardens
5873 Oliver Avenue SW
Cokato, MN 55321
Catalog $2

Carroll Gardens
444 E. Main Strett
Westminster, MD 21158
Catalog $3

Klehm Nursery
4210 N. Duncan Road
Champaign, IL 61821
Catalog $4

Milaeger's Gardens
4838 Douglas Avenue
Racine, WI 53402-2498
Catalog $1

Andre Viette Farm & Nursery
Route 1, Box 16
Fishersville, VA 22939
Catalog $3

Wayside Gardens
P.O. Box 1
Hodges, SC 29695-0001
Catalog $1

White Flower Farm
P.O. Box 50
Litchfield, CT 06759-0050
Free catalog

Mail-order perennial plant specialists:

DAYLILIES:

American Daylily & Perennials
P.O. Box 210
Grain Valley, MO 64029
Catalog $5

Bloomingfields Farm
Route 55
Gaylordsville, CT 06755-0005
Free catalog

Daylily Discounters
1 Daylily Plaza
Alachua, FL 32615
Catalog $2

Daylily World
P.O. Box 1612
Sanford, FL 32772-1612
Catalog $5

Louisiana Nursery
Route 7, Box 43
Opelousas, LA 70570
Daylily catalog $3

Oakes Daylilies
8204 Monday Road
Corryton, TN 37721
Catalog $2

Saxton Gardens
1 First Street
Saratoga Springs, NY 12866
Catalog $1

R. Seawright
P.O. Box 733
Carlisle, MA 01741-0733
Catalog $2

Snow Creek Daylily Gardens
330 P Street
Port Townsend, WA 98368
Catalog $2

Tranquil Lake Nursery
45 River Street
Rehoboth, MA 02769-1395
Catalog $1

MUMS:

Huff's Garden Mums
710 Tuniatta St.
Burlington, KS 66839-0187
Free catalog

King's Mums
P.O. Box 368
Clements, CA 95227
Catalog $2

Sunnyslope Gardens
8638 Huntington Drive
San Gabriel, CA 91775
Free catalog

PEONIES:

A&D Peony Nursery
6808 180th Street SE
Snohomish, WA 98290
Catalog $2

Brand Peony Farm
P.O. Box 842
St. Cloud, MN 56302
Catalog $1

Klehm Nursery
4210 N. Duncan Road
Champaign, IL 61821
Catalog $4

The New Peony Farm
P.O. Box 18235
St. Paul, MN 55118
Free catalog

Reath's Nursery
County Road 577, Box N-195
Vulcan, MN 49892
Catalog $1

Australian Sources

Country Farm Perennials
RSD Laings Road
Nayook VIC 3821

Cox's Nursery
RMB 216 Oaks Road
Thrilmere NSW 2572
Honeysuckle Cottage Nursery
Lot 35 Bowen Mountain Road
Bowen Mountain via Grosevale
NSW 2753

Canadian Sources

Corn Hill Nursery Ltd.
RR 5
Petitcodiac NB EOA 2HO

Ferncliff Gardens
SS 1
Mission, British Columbia
V2V 5V6

Stirling Perennials
RR 1
Morpeth, Ontario
N0P 1X0